9-23-8

THE COMPLETE GUIDE TO GOOGLE ADVERTISING: INCLUDING TIPS, TRICKS, & STRATEGIES TO CREATE A WINNING ADVERTISING PLAN

Copyright © 2007 by Atlantic Publishing Group, Inc.
1405 SW 6th Ave. • Ocala, Florida 34471 • 800-814-1132 • 352-622-1875–Fax
Web site: www.atlantic-pub.com • E-mail: sales@atlantic-pub.com
SAN Number: 268-1250

ISBN-13: 978-1-60138-045-6   ISBN-10: 1-60138-045-3

Library of Congress Cataloging-in-Publication Data

Brown, Bruce C. (Bruce Cameron), 1965-
  The complete guide to Google advertising : including tips, tricks, & strategies to create a winning advertising plan / by Bruce C. Brown.

     p. cm.
ISBN-13: 978-1-60138-045-6 (alk. paper)
ISBN-10: 1-60138-045-3 (alk. paper)
 1. Internet marketing--Handbooks, manuals, etc. 2. Internet advertising--Handbooks, manuals, etc. 3. Google--Handbooks, manuals, etc. 4. Web sites--Design--Handbooks, manuals, etc. 5. Web search engines--Handbooks, manuals, etc. I. Title. II. Title: Guide to Google advertising. III. Title: Google advertising.

HF5415.1265.B7643 2007
659.14'4--dc22
                        2007033293

D1331245

Printed on Recycled Paper

INTERIOR LAYOUT DESIGN: Vickie Taylor • vtaylor@atlantic-pub.com

Printed in the United States

THE COMPLETE GUIDE TO GOOGLE ADVERTISING

Including Tips, Tricks, & Strategies to

Create a Winning Advertising Plan

BY BRUCE C. BROWN

We recently lost our beloved pet "Bear," who was not only
our best and dearest friend but also the "Vice President of
Sunshine" here at Atlantic Publishing. He did not receive
a salary but worked tirelessly 24 hours a day to please his
parents. Bear was a rescue dog that turned around and
showered myself, my wife Sherri, his grandparents Jean, Bob
and Nancy and every person and animal he met (maybe not
rabbits) with friendship and love. He made a lot of people
smile every day.

We wanted you to know that a portion of the profits of this
book will be donated to The Humane Society of
the United States.

–Douglas & Sherri Brown

THE HUMANE SOCIETY
OF THE UNITED STATES ©

The human-animal bond is as old as human history. We cherish our animal companions for their unconditional affection and acceptance. We feel a thrill when we glimpse wild creatures in their natural habitat or in our own backyard.

Unfortunately, the human-animal bond has at times been weakened. Humans have exploited some animal species to the point of extinction.

The Humane Society of the United States makes a difference in the lives of animals here at home and worldwide. The HSUS is dedicated to creating a world where our relationship with animals is guided by compassion. We seek a truly humane society in which animals are respected for their intrinsic value, and where the human-animal bond is strong.

Want to help animals? We have plenty of suggestions. Adopt a pet from a local shelter, join The Humane Society and be a part of our work to help companion animals and wildlife. You will be funding our educational, legislative, investigative and outreach projects in the U.S. and across the globe.

Or perhaps you'd like to make a memorial donation in honor of a pet, friend or relative? You can through our Kindred Spirits program. And if you'd like to contribute in a more structured way, our Planned Giving Office has suggestions about estate planning, annuities, and even gifts of stock that avoid capital gains taxes.

Maybe you have land that you would like to preserve as a lasting habitat for wildlife. Our Wildlife Land Trust can help you. Perhaps the land you want to share is a backyard—that's enough. Our Urban Wildlife Sanctuary Program will show you how to create a habitat for your wild neighbors.

So you see, it's easy to help animals. And The HSUS is here to help.

The Humane Society of the United States
2100 L Street NW
Washington, DC 20037
202-452-1100
www.hsus.org

CONTENTS

CHAPTER 2: HISTORY OF GOOGLE & ONLINE ADVERTISING......................23

CHAPTER 3: DEVELOPING AN ONLINE MARKETING PLAN 35

CHAPTER 4: HOW TO GENERATE WEB SITE TRAFFIC WITH AND WITHOUT GOOGLE...........................45

CHAPTER 5: INTRODUCTION TO PAY-PER-CLICK ADVERTISING.................61

CHAPTER 6: USING GOOGLE ADWORDS.................71

CHAPTER 7: HOW TO CHOOSE EFFECTIVE KEYWORDS & KEY PHRASES 105

CHAPTER 8: INCREASE PROFITS WITH GOOGLE ADSENSE 121

CHAPTER 9: HOW TO IDENTIFY & COMBAT PAY-PER-CLICK FRAUD 137

CHAPTER 10: OPTIMIZE YOUR WEB SITE FOR SEARCH ENGINES 155

FOREWORD

By Paul J. Bliss, III

Google. That word is synonymous with intelligence, information, speed, results, innovation, traffic, and money.

No one knows the "secret sauce" for Google's algorithm except for the creators and the guardians of it. Therefore, we can only make educated guesses about the techniques that work, and we can only use simple logic to determine what Google will value and rank in their results.

Long gone are the days of keyword stuffing your meta tags to get top rankings. To get rankings today, you must engage in a mind set equal to that of a field commander. Every word and phrase involves competition. Every part of a Web site must be optimized. Since people consume content in different ways, every podcast, video, image, and page of your Web site needs to be optimized.

Anything that exists in a digital format can be found and ranked in Google. And those who know this can take advantage of the almost endless opportunities that exist for those who take the time to craft and create content. Knowing the correct phrases to pursue makes all the difference.

Search engine optimization (SEO) is not for the weak of heart nor the impatient. It will take time. Mistakes will be made. But keep the long-term goal in sight and you can achieve these results.

Google also means opportunity. History has never seen something as powerful as the Internet, and there is no other medium where the "Little Guy" can not only compete, but beat the "Big Boys." Many times the online competition is vastly different from the regional brick-and-mortar businesses.

Google is the only business that wants you to leave their site. The faster you find a relevant hit for your search, the better their algorithm has worked. By being that relevant hit, the Web site and Google benefit; the Web site gets a targeted user, and Google gains more trust by delivering great results.

The race to get ranked in Google accelerates every day. Just being in the race will get some results, but knowing what Google looks for and knowing what the algorithm wants is your key to success.

The information contained in this book will give you the history of this great company and provide you with key insights on how you can take this knowledge and apply the techniques and ideas found within to catapult your Web site to the top.

To your online success!

Paul J. Bliss III, Owner
SEOforGoogle.com

SEO FOR GOOGLE

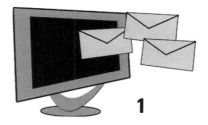

INTRODUCTION

Google is the number one search engine in the world. It is also the world's most popular search engine. This book will reveal the secrets of Google and provide you with the insight, tools, and knowledge to use Google to dramatically expand your marketing campaigns. One of the most amazing benefits of Google is that many of its applications are entirely free. I will provide you with the tips, tricks, and practical advice to drive your Web site to the top rankings in Google, without breaking the bank. Obtaining high search engine rankings is a combination of many factors, starting with overall Web site design and culminating in an effective Web site marketing strategy that maximizes your potential for high rankings and increased revenues or Web site traffic, while balancing the constraints of often limited resources and budgets. My goal is to reveal how you can use Google to increase revenue while managing limited resources, budgets, and technical expertise.

In this book, we will discuss, in great detail, pay-per-click advertising (PPC) and other marketing techniques that can be used in conjunction with Google. Pay-per-click advertising is simply a marketing and advertising technique in which you are allowed (typically at no cost) to place advertisements on Web sites and major search engines' results pages. We will discuss all aspects of the PPC marketing campaign, including all the relevant methodology to ensure your campaign maximizes overall effectiveness while staying within budget. With PPC advertising, you simply pay for the "clicks." A click is when a Web site browser sees your advertisement and clicks on it. They will be taken to your Web site where they will, in theory, buy a product from you. You pay for that "click" based on a pre-determined dollar amount per click (cost per click), regardless of whether that "click" actually results in a sale on your Web site. You are simply paying for the clicks generated by placing your advertisement on other business's Web sites. You will see an increase in Web site, generated through the advertisement for your Web site; however, there is no guarantee that PPC advertising campaigns will increase sales or revenue. That is the reason why this book takes you through each step of the process and maximizes your potential for success.

In my book *The Ultimate Guide to Search Engine Marketing: Pay Per Click Advertising Secrets Revealed* we delved deep into all aspects of pay-per-click marketing and will do so in this book as it is related specifically to Google. However, this book is much more than another book about pay-per-click marketing. We will cover all aspects of Google marketing, from how you can use it for your company to how you can realize dramatic increases in revenue and Web site traffic. In addition, I will provide you with industry leading tips and secrets, along with the little known secrets of Google.

WHO IS THIS BOOK FOR?

This book is written for anyone who has a Web site, is considering developing a Web site, companies with an established online presence who wish to expand their marketing campaigns, for the small business, large business, and sole proprietor, as well as anyone else who is interested in making money, increasing Web site traffic, driving up revenue, and improving the financial posture of their organization. This book is a practical guide for how to harness the power of Google. As with all my books, my immediate goal is to inform, educate, and provide you with relevant ideas which you can immediately implement, all at little or no cost. This book is the ideal Google guide for businesses with limited budgets, minimal marketing plans, and limited technical support staffs.

HOW THIS BOOK IS ORGANIZED

Each chapter is packed with relevant content, advice, tips, and strategies for Google success, and the chapters are broken down in the following manner:

History of Google & Online Advertising

This chapter provides you with a condensed version of the history of Google and how it grew to be the leading search engine in the world. Additionally, you will be presented with the evolution of online marketing and the different types of campaigns/marketing strategies employed by Web site operators to promote their business through search engines, free marketing, and pay-per-click marketing programs.

Developing an Online Marketing Plan

Included here is a brief presentation and review of how to develop a marketing plan for an online business and incorporate Google's wide variety of functionality into a successful business plan.

How to Generate Web Site Traffic With (and Without) Google

This chapter provides tips and tricks on how to generate Web site traffic with (and without) Google, increase visibility in search engines, and improve Web site rankings in all major search engines. This chapter concentrates primarily on media exposure and other techniques you can use in conjunction with your Google marketing campaigns.

Introduction to Pay-Per-Click Advertising

Here you will find a general overview of pay-per-click (PPC) advertising, how it works, how it compares to other marketing techniques, and how to effectively design a PPC campaign for maximum success. An in-depth introduction to how PPC works, comparison to other marketing techniques, an in-depth walk through from start to finish of how PPC works, what happens when a site visitor clicks on an advertisement, how it is tracked, and how this generates traffic and site revenue will also be covered.

Using Google AdWords

This chapter includes a comprehensive introduction to Google AdWords, Google's PPC application. Also included are instructions for detailed setup, campaign design, and management of all your Google AdWords campaigns. We delve deep into Google advertising campaigns and reveal a multitude of tips, tricks, and secrets on how to maximize the effectiveness of your campaigns.

How to Choose Effective Keywords and Key Phrases and Budget for a Pay-Per-Click Advertising Campaign

This is often the most neglected area in developing a PPC campaign and the biggest factor in improving a campaign. We will discuss how to effectively choose keywords and key phrases to maximize the effectiveness of PPC marketing campaigns. I will include an explanation of how to use available tools to evaluate keywords, effectiveness, and pricing schemes for maximum keyword cost per click effectiveness in relation to overall campaign budgets.

Increase Profits with Google Adsense

Here you will find an introduction to the Google Adsense program, which is another opportunity for you to generate income by allowing other advertisers to place PPC ads on your Web site. This no-cost Google program is an excellent tool to generate revenue at no cost.

How to Identify and Combat Fraud with Google AdWords

This chapter provides you with a comprehensive guide to help you understand fraud, identify it, and combat it and preserve the integrity and financial stability of your pay-per-click campaign. Fraud is the number one problem facing pay-per-click marketing campaigns, and we show you how to be successful in combating it in conjunction with Google AdWords.

Optimize Your Web Site for Google Search Engine

Here you will find a general guide to designing your site for maximum search engine optimization, as well as tips and tricks to garner the most from site visitors to increase revenues and Web site design effectiveness. A key area of emphasis is how to improve site design to maximize revenue.

Google Base and Froogle

Google Base is a place where you can easily submit all types of online and offline content. We will show you how to list your products on Google Base and Froogle and dramatically expand your marketplace.

Pay-Per-Click Case Studies

Do not just take my word for it that Google pay-per-click marketing can fuel an enormous increase in online sales, generate substantial Web site traffic, and increase your potential customer base. Read the results of others who have ventured into pay-per-click marketing and succeeded.

Advice from Google Industry Experts

We have compiled the best advice, tips, and suggestions from industry leaders who have achieved enormous success using Google marketing tools and through the Google search engine.

Recommended Reference Library

This is my list of must-have reference books to help you develop your portfolio of success in your online marketing ventures. I have provided you with recommended sources for pay-per-click providers, affiliate programs, and other useful sources for your online business.

Glossary

Here you will find a glossary of terms and definitions.

WHAT YOU WILL LEARN

I will provide you with the tools and knowledge to unlock the secrets of Google and enable you to use the Internet to its fullest potential to promote, advertise, and market your business in a cost-effective campaign designed to increase revenue. The Internet is the ultimate marketing tool – giving you immediate access to billions of people worldwide. By implementing marketing campaigns, such as pay-per-click and understanding the wide range of applications available for your business through Google, you will develop a solid marketing plan which is both efficient and cost-effective. You will benefit from search engine technology in which your customers are actively being fed links back to your Web site. After reading this book and applying the principles and techniques contained within you will empower your business and your business's Web site to operate a cost-effective and highly successful marketing campaign, ensuring the maximum return on investment through pay-per-click and other marketing programs.

I provide you with all the tools and steps that you need to take to maximize and harness the power of the Internet to promote and market your business and products through Google, as well as the formulas for success in developing your overall Web site strategy, design philosophy, search engine optimization, and alternative marketing strategies. If you follow the guiding principles contained in this book, you will be successful in harnessing the impressive power, flexibility, and cost-effectiveness of Google.

Every topic covered in his book can be exclusively designed, implemented, and managed by you. You do not need to be a professional Web designer or hire an expensive marketing firm to promote and market your online business.

The concepts in this book are simple and will help you reach your customers and potential customers in a way that you could not previously. Google applications enable your potential customers to seek you out through no cost ad placements on Web sites and in search engine results, as well as by providing you with a no-cost solution to promoting your products worldwide. We designed this book for the small business, which does not have a large (or any) information technology or Web design staff and is limited on technology budget and knowledge. If you are the owner, proprietor, or manager of a traditional brick and mortar or online business and you need to implement successful marketing campaigns such as pay-per-click advertising and harness the power of Google to dramatically expand your customer sales base, this book is for you. I will show you how to save thousands of dollars in costs compared with traditional marketing programs, such as flyers, postcards, or other forms of offline or postal advertising. These antiquated methods only reach a small customer base, are costly to produce and distribute, and fail to generate a return. Google lets you do it faster, better, and for significantly less investment in time, resources, and money.

The key principle to remember with Google marketing tools is that you never pay for ad space, list ranking, search engine ranking, or to promote your products. In short, you are not paying up front fees with no promise of a return on investment. You are employing the power of Google's tools through effective online marketing to draw thousands of potential new customers to your Web site every day.

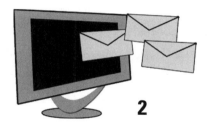

2

HISTORY OF GOOGLE & ONLINE ADVERTISING

Google has an interesting and inspiring history. The company had humble beginnings but has grown into an industry giant.

In 1998, Larry Page and Sergey Brin founded Google while they were students at Stanford. The search engine originally began as a research project designed to demonstrate how a search engine that was capable of analyzing the relationship between Web sites would be more effective than one that simply ranked sites according to the number of times the search term appeared on the page. After Page and Brin used the site as their thesis, Google was incorporated in 1998. The company quickly outgrew the garage in Menlo Park, California, where it started, as well as its offices in Palo Alto and two other sites. Currently, Google resides in a complex located in Mountain View, California; the complex has since acquired the nickname "Googleplex."

Two years later in 2000, Google began to sell advertisements associated with keywords. These ads were text-based in order to keep with the company's simple design. The company has continued to grow, acquiring such small companies as Pyra Labs, Upstartle, YouTube, and DoubleClick and has begun to experiment in new markets, including radio and print, by purchasing radio advertising company dMarc and selling ads from its advertisers in select print publications.

In addition to these ventures, Google has launched several of its own applications. These include AdWords and AdSense, two advertising programs, Gmail, a Web-based e-mail client, Google Video, Google Earth, and Google Apps Premium Edition, a software suite designed to rival Microsoft Office. All these features have combined to make Google the most used search engine on the Internet.

Wikipedia provides a much more in-depth history of the company, which can be found at **http://en.wikipedia.org/wiki/Google** and **http://en.wikipedia.org/wiki/History_of_Google**.

Google truly represents the American dream and epitomizes ingenuity, entrepreneurship, and the rags to riches success story.

DEVELOPMENT OF ONLINE MARKETING

Online marketing schemes have been around since the invention and creation of the World Wide Web. As Web sites were developed into online businesses targeting increased revenues for traditional brick and mortar businesses, the importance and prominence of online marketing became a dominating force in the industry. Today there are literally hundreds of thousands of businesses that exist solely on the Internet and do not maintain a traditional retail store. Therefore, online marketing, pay-per-click campaigns, and other enterprising marketing schemes have become increasingly prevalent and extraordinarily competitive. To fully understand how to take advantage of Google, it is important to understand the history of online marketing and the variety of Web-based marketing techniques deployed in the past and present.

Marketing and advertising a traditional brick and mortar business is a costly venture. Postage and mailing costs are high, and return rates on mailings are often a dismal 1 percent of the total mailing or less. Over 200 million Americans went online in 2005, and nearly one billion people worldwide used the Internet during this same period. Internet access grew more than 107 percent in 2005 in the United States and more than 165 percent worldwide.

According to Internet World Stats (**www.internetworldstats.com**), worldwide Internet use ballooned a staggering 189 percent between 2000 and 2005, caused by the rest of the world's population catching up with the previous growth seen in the United States. Growth in the Middle East exploded by nearly 500 percent during this same period.

INTERNET MARKETING

According to Wikipedia, Internet marketing is defined as a "component of electronic commerce." This particular form of marketing often includes customer service, sales, public relations, information management, and market research. The growth in Internet usage has caused a reciprocal growth in Internet marketing. In the early 1990s, Internet marketing was a new frontier in advertising and sales. Commercial Web sites were nothing more than a corporate public relations presence with generalized information about a company and/or its products and services. As technology and the understanding of the HyperText Markup Language (HTML) improved, the predominant language for the creation of Web sites improved and commercial Web sites evolved into little more than online brochures and catalogs of corporate product lines. These were designed to allow a potential customer to do research and explore the products online, and then go to the brick and mortar retail outlet or place a phone order. Since credit card payment processing was readily available in retail outlets and there was no security available online for the processing of credit cards, online sales were minimal. Thousands of companies allowed customers to place credit card orders using basic HTML order forms, which captured the un-encrypted credit card information, recklessly sending potentially harmful personal financial information throughout the Internet. As awareness of credit card fraud and theft increased, savvy Web customers refrained from placing credit card orders online in fear of comprising personal financial data.

Everything changed with the development of encryption methods and secure site technology. Data could be captured securely and transmitted over the Internet in an encrypted format to protect data online. Since the development of encryption technology, online purchasing has exploded and is expected to grow exponentially in the future. Small startup companies like Amazon.com have grown into online sales powerhouses.

Atlantic Publishing Company (**www.atlantic-pub.com**) is a classic example of how the Internet has positively affected business and marketing operations. In the mid-1990s Atlantic Publishing Company embraced the Internet with a basic Web site, featuring a full list of their product lines with pricing and ordering information. The Web site featured an online order form, which required the user to manually enter the items they wanted, manually calculate the item costs and totals, and was sent via a secure Web page to the corporate headquarters for processing. Today, Atlantic Publishing Company features a state-of-the-art Web site boasting a full featured shopping cart, secure online order processing, advanced search capabilities, and simplified navigation. The Internet transformed them from a catalog-based business into an online publishing powerhouse, producing more than 50 original publications in 2006 on a wide-range of topics including food service, restaurant management, real estate, human resources, customer service, Internet sales and marketing, and personal finance.

INTERNET ADVERTISING

Advertising may be defined as any paid form of communication about an organization, its products, and/or services by an identified and typically paid sponsor. As we have previously discussed, online marketing and advertising campaigns were designed to replicate existing advertising, which was intended for traditional advertising outlets such as print media (newspapers, books, and magazines), as well as multimedia advertising, which includes television and radio. With the expansion of the Internet, the potential impact on customer sales base and revenues was realized and online advertising was born.

In 2007, online advertising and marketing has matured and become very refined, largely due to Google. We have moved past most of the dynamic and revolutionary changes in the evolution of online advertising and are now seeking to refine existing advertising techniques to garner the most out of a companies marketing investment. Technology, population growth, and the increasing number of households with broadband Internet access have pushed advances in technology in the online advertising world, generating billions of dollars in sales annually. The use of online advertising as the primary advertising form within corporations is overtaking traditional advertising means.

The potential for developing highly innovative and unique advertisements which draw in potential customers is practically limitless. As the Internet grew in size and popularity the amount of money spent on online advertising increased dramatically, as did the desire to develop a variety of cost-effective advertising methods which promised a high return for low investment.

TYPES OF ONLINE ADVERTISEMENTS

Three major areas which continue to own the majority of the online marketing share are:

- Paid search advertisement (pay-per-click)

- Banner advertisements

- Classified ads

We will discuss each of these in this book as they relate to Google, but will concentrate on pay-per-click advertising since this is one of the best products Google offers through its Google AdWords program. Additionally, we will discuss a variety of other advertising methods and Google tools, which will help promote your online business at little or no cost.

UNDERSTANDING BANNER ADVERTISING

Banner advertising is simply a form of online advertising in which Web developers embed an advertisement into the HTML code of a Web page. The idea is that the banner advertisement will catch the attention of Web site visitors, and they will click on the ad to get more information about the products or services advertised. When clicked, the banner ad will take the Web browser to the Web site operated by the advertiser. A banner ad can be created in a variety of formats, such as .GIF, .JPG, or .PNG. Banner ads can be static images or employ a variety of scripting code, Java, or other advanced techniques, such as animated gifs or rollover images, to create rotating banner advertisements which change every few seconds. Over the past five years Shockwave and Macromedia Flash technology have become increasingly popular by incorporating animation, sound, and action into banner advertisements. Banner ads are created in a variety of shapes and sizes depending on the site content and design and are designed to be placed unobtrusively in the "white" space available in a traditionally designed Web page.

When a page is loaded into a Web browser such as Microsoft Internet

Explorer or Mozilla's Firefox, the banner is loaded onto the page, creating what is called an "impression." An impression simply means that the Web page containing the advertisement was loaded and potentially viewed by someone who is browsing that Web site. Impressions allow advertisers to track how many visitors loaded that particular page (and banner ad) in a set period of time. If the impression count is low, it is logical that the click through rate and subsequent sales will also be extremely low. When the Web site visitor clicks on the banner advertisement, the browser is navigated to the Web site, which is linked to the banner ad, and the Web site is loaded into the browser. The process of a site visitor clicking on a banner ad with their mouse is commonly called a "click through." Click throughs are important to advertisers because they track how many visitors actually clicked on a particular banner ad and how many resultant sales were generated by the banner ad in a set period of time. Unfortunately, a high click through rate does not necessarily guarantee high sales. Banner ads can be static (embedded in the actual HTML page) by the Webmaster or may be "served" through a central server, which enables advertisers to display a wide variety of banner ads on thousands of Web sites with minimal effort.

As we have already discussed, most banner ads currently work on a per-click system, where the advertiser pays for each click on the banner ad, regardless of whether that click results in a sale. Originally, advertisers simply paid for the ad space on a Web site, often for a preset period of time, such as a week or month, and hoped that someone would see the banner ad and click on it to visit their Web site. Banner advertising is typically a very low cost investment per click (usually under ten cents per click) and the banner provider or hosting company then bills the advertiser on a pre-determined basis. The key difference between banner advertising and pay-per-click advertising is that banner advertisements are placed in the content of Web pages, while pay-per-click advertising is not image based and may be dynamically generated based on search results.

Banner advertising was extremely popular in the 1990s and early 2000s and is still commonly used today; however, it is less effective and even less popular than other advertising techniques, such as pay-per-click advertising. Banner advertising is designed to inform potential customers or consumers about the products or services offered by the advertiser, just like traditional print advertising, but they offer the advantage of allowing advertisers to track individual statistics and performance at a level not possible with print media advertising.

When banner ads were originally created, they were highly successful; however, as Web surfers became Web savvy, these ads were viewed as annoying and often distracted from the actual Web site content. It was not uncommon to have Web pages loaded with hundreds of banner ads on a single page or Web sites which were nothing more than placeholders for hundreds of banner ads. Today the standard has improved dramatically, and you will not find more than one or two unobtrusive banner advertisements on any Web page. Additionally, Web browsers such as Microsoft's Internet Explorer and Mozilla's Firefox contain built in pop-up blockers designed to suppress many banner advertisements. If you choose to pursue banner ads on your Web site or through others to generate revenue and traffic, you will want to concentrate on the chapter related to search engine optimization, as Google does not offer any tools directly related to banner advertising. On the other hand, we will explore Google AdWords (Google's pay-per-click marketing tool) in great detail in this book.

UNDERSTANDING STATIC VERSUS DYNAMIC

In the early days of Web site development, Web sites were "static" in content and were easy to build and maintain, but did not offer an "interactive" experience. Internet advertising was primarily limited to static or server-based banner advertising. The development of database driven Web sites created an entirely new experience for the Web site visitor, enabling them to enter data into a Web site and receive dynamically generated content based on their query. An example of this is **www.google.com** or **www.tbo.com/classifieds/**, which enables the site visitor to search on any topic they wish to see results generated for.

The development of Web portals, such as **www.yahoo.com** and **www. msn.com**, enabled Web visitors to personalize their Web browsing experience. Personalization allows a Web site visitor to enter information such as name, age, zip code, and other personal preferences to dynamically deliver customized Web content based on the chosen preferences. More advanced Web sites, such as **Amazon.com**, can make recommendations to site visitors based on their profile and preferences, thereby potentially increasing sales and revenue.

With most users today surfing the Web on high-speed broadband, Web site developers have been developing what is known as "rich media." Rich media is advertisements geared toward high-speed Internet browsers and can display video, audio, music, animations, and special effects. The addition of flashy advertising to interactivity has completed the online experience, as consumers receive interactive and often entertaining advertisements disguised as music videos, games, and other interactive content, all with the ultimate goal of producing increased Web site traffic and Internet sales. Although rich media may be the banner ad of the future, it still has quite a ways to go to replace traditional banner advertising.

The Web site **www.ecommercetimes.com** recently listed some statistics pertaining to Internet advertising, including a survey conducted by Nielsen. In the survey, which was released for the week ending August 6, 2006, Nielsen reported that, of an estimated 57.6 million impressions, a mere 1.2 percent were rich media. Those with the most were "compound image/text ads with more than 16 million impressions (27.9 percent), followed by sponsored search links with 14.6 million impressions (25.3

percent), standard gif/jpeg with 13.6 million impressions (23.7 percent), and Flash ads with 12.8 million (22 percent)." However, it is estimated that 39 percent of Internet ad spending is expected to be on rich media.

Rich media has evolved in the past year into the recycling of television advertisements and the incorporating of full TV commercials into the Internet. Floating and expanding banners are increasingly popular and equally frustrating to the Web site visitor. Floating and expanding ads utilize motion and appear to float across the screen, blocking the view of the actual Web site content and often require a click to close the ad; however, most are set to disappear after a set time interval. Sound embedded in banner advertising is becoming increasingly visible, where sound bites are launched with a Web site as an additional attempt to attract site visitors to click on the specific Web site banner. Podcasts, blogs, and RSS broadcasts have become extremely popular in recent years. It is anticipated the more than 12 million Americans will access podcasts alone in 2007. Large advertisers such as Best Buy, Acura, and Volvo are already sponsoring podcasts. Mobile or cellular marketing advertising is growing as the population increases its use of iPods, MP3 players, cell phones, Blackberries and Treos. The recent purchase of YouTube by Google will likely have an impact on the explosive growth of rich media on the Internet.

Pay-per-click advertising is thought to be the most efficient and effective method of online advertising today — enabling you to quickly promote your business online in a cost-effective program. Additionally, it is one of the secrets to getting your Web site listed at the top of major search engines without having to do any search engine optimization, although I cannot emphasize the importance of search engine optimization on your overall marketing and advertising campaigns and search engine visibility.

With the background history I have provided on Google and online marketing and advertising, you should have a good understanding of the variety of advertisement campaigns in existence. You are now ready to begin developing an online marketing plan. By exploring each chapter of this book, you will gain insight, and you will be provided with tools, advice, and success stories to ensure your campaign is effective, attainable, and flexible.

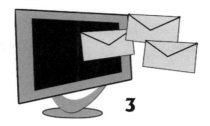

DEVELOPING AN ONLINE MARKETING PLAN

An essential step before you begin to implement Google marketing on your Web site is to craft a well-thought out marketing plan. If you think your business is too small to require such a plan, think again. An online marketing plan is critical in mapping out your future marketing goals. Writing a marketing plan is a fairly straight forward process which requires you to set clear objectives and describe how you will achieve them.

A marketing plan must be achievable, realistic, cost-effective, measurable, and flexible. With Google, the process of creating an online marketing plan is simplified, since Google offers a wide array of products which will assist you in developing a comprehensive marking plan.

Your marketing plan may consist of:

- Market analysis

- Business objectives

- Marketing strategies

- Steps to achieving business objectives

- Realistic budget

- Realistic timeline

PERFORMING A MARKET ANALYSIS

A marketing plan is a living document. You must be flexible based on budget, competition, and business objectives, as well as internal and external influences. Essentially, market analysis helps you determine if there is a need for your supplies or services. Understanding the marketplace, the desire for your products, and competition helps you determine the key information that will be essential to establishing a successful business in a competitive environment. If there is no need for your products, you will likely fail unless you establish your presence in the marketplace. Likewise, if there is a high level of competition, you must develop a marketing plan that allows you to compete in regard to product, quality, availability, or price. Knowing what the marketplace needs and how it is currently serviced provides you with key information.

Statistics prove that up to 50 percent of a product's price is spent on marketing. Welcome to the world of Google, where you can significantly reduce this to just a few percentage points or less.

Although marketing and marketing analysis seem similar, they should not be confused with one another. When we refer to marketing we are talking about everything done to promote a company's product or service. On the other hand, a marketing analysis is a study of the target audience, the competition, and the demand for a company's product or service.

The following questions will help you to perform a basic market analysis:

- What market am I trying to enter?

- What is my current competition?

- How successful is my competition?

- What percentage of the market share does my competition hold?

- Is the market flooded or open?

- What is the market size? Is there room to grow?

- Is there stability in the market or is it volatile?

- How are my competitors marketing their goods or services?

- What do customers seek in regards to my products? What is most valuable to them?

- What are customers willing to pay for my products or services?

- What do I offer that my competition does not?

You should analyze current or previous marketing strategies, as well as those of your competition, both successful and unsuccessful. Understanding failure is as important as understanding success factors. These questions may help you analyze your potential for success in a competitive marketplace:

- Am I offering a new product line, new service, or unique product?

- What marketing strategies have I (or my competition) used successfully? What was unsuccessful? Have I used online marketing in the past? What was the success rate or return on investment?

- Have I evaluated the results of previous marketing plans (print advertising, pay-per-click, e-mail marketing, and so forth? What was the impact on sales?

- Are we using any strategies currently?

- What strategies are my competitors using currently?

- How much money do I have for marketing in my current budget? How much am I currently spending? How much was my marketing budget in the past?

- Why would someone choose our product over our competition?

- What do we do to distinguish ourselves from our competition?

- Why would someone trust us more than our competition?

- Who are our customers?

- Where do our customers come from?

You must perform what is known as primary and secondary research. Primary research includes phone interviews, surveys, Web-based surveys, and focus groups. Primary research is the most current information available. Secondary research is data which has already been collected for other purposes, but may assist you with your market research. Examples of secondary research may be libraries, blogs, or other online resources.

*Market Analysis Information from: **http://www.va-interactive.com/ inbusiness/editorial/sales/ibt/market_analysis.html***

Since we are concentrating on Google advertising and your primary area of concern is competition from other online businesses, it makes perfect sense that your market analysis may be performed by using the Internet.

The Internet contains a wealth of analytical information and may prove to be your greatest ally in performing market analysis.

ESTABLISHING BUSINESS OBJECTIVES

The sad fact is that nearly 50 percent of new businesses will fail within four years. This is also true for online businesses; however, you do have some distinct advantages over traditional brick and mortar businesses, as well as some overarching negatives. You may not have as many employees, less building space, and, most importantly, less overhead. However, without the traditional storefront, you also do not have a physical presence; instead you have a virtual presence. This is fine if potential customers can find you. If they cannot find you, you will fail. I highly recommend reading my previous books, such as *How to Use the Internet to Advertise, Promote and Market Your Business or Web Site with Little or No Money, The Complete Guide to E-mail Marketing: How to Create Successful, Spam-Free Campaigns to Reach Your Target Audience and Increase Sales*, and *The Ultimate Guide to Search Engine Marketing: Pay Per Click Advertising Secrets Revealed*, for additional information about online marketing. Pay special attention to search engine optimization; without a well-designed Web site, you may find that customers cannot find your Web site.

Let us look at how to establish your business objectives. You need to develop a long-term business plan that will map out your path toward success. You may have heard this called a strategic plan or strategic goals. This plan is simply your goals, objectives, and timelines in a written format. This document is intended to be "living," and can easily be adjusted based on the current operating environment. You will need to complete your market analysis to assist in preparing your long-term business objectives. You may be asking, "How can I know what my objectives and timelines are when I don't know how successful I will be in the future or what will happen to my company in the next few years?" The point of business objectives is not to predict the future, but to establish the desired course of action, setting strategic goals along the way. Business objectives may be things like Establish Web presence by July 1, Develop Pay-per-click marketing campaign by August 1, Implement e-mail marketing campaign by September 1, and so on. Your objectives should be attainable and must be measurable so you can evaluate your success in meeting (or failing to meet) them.

You should first perform a comprehensive evaluation of your current business state. What have you accomplished; what have you not? Are you profitable or operating at a loss? What and who is your competition? What are the industry trends in relation to your products or services (i.e. changing technology)? Use resources, such as the Small Business Administration (**www.sba.gov/library/pubs.html**), the chamber of commerce, industry associations, and the local library, to help you research and establish your business objectives.

Document your initial findings and business objectives. Review goals with your employees (they may provide input or ideas which you have not thought about). Ensure that your plan addresses all aspects of your organization, such as sales, marketing, human resources, advertising, customer service, information technology, and so forth.

Develop a mission statement for your company. A mission statement captures your organization's purpose, customer orientation, and business philosophy. Share your mission statement with employees and post it in a prominent place. You must have employees "buy in" to your mission statement if you want them to share your vision and help you achieve your strategic objectives.

Ensure that you update your business objectives at least annually, perhaps even semi-annually, during your initial operating years.

ESTABLISHING MARKETING STRATEGIES

This book will be an invaluable guide to harnessing the power of Google as you design and implement your marketing strategy and plans.

You must establish a clearly defined, written strategy, and marketing plan for your online business. You must consider all marketing strategies and implement those which are most relevant to your business operations and offer the most potential for increased customer base and return on investment. Your marketing strategy must be realistic and measurable. If you do not measure the results of your marketing campaign, you cannot evaluate their effectiveness or be ready to implement a shift in strategy. At a minimum, your marketing strategy should include:

- Profile of the target consumer

- Competitive market analysis

- Distribution plans for your products

- Product price strategy

- Advertising budget

- Advertising and marketing strategy analysis to evaluate potential methods

- Your corporation vision and business objectives

- Brand uniqueness or image for your products

- Evaluation of your products and services

- Distinction of your company/products from competitors

Implement and evaluate your marketing strategy as it relates to achieving your corporate business objectives. Keep in mind that some marketing plans may take significant time and investment — think long term and do not be quick to change your objectives because you are not realizing the goals in your specified timelines. Be flexible, but allow your marketing strategies time to grow and mature.

Throughout each chapter of this book I will provide you with Google specific marketing ideas for your company. Google is the market leader in pay-per-click and other marketing campaigns, and as the world's most popular and powerful search engine, it is the one you want to see your Web site ranked high on. I will help you achieve that, but keep in mind that Google is not the only player in town. You may want to expand your marketing plan to achieve success in other major search engines such as Yahoo and MSN. By implementing good search engine optimization techniques, as provided in this book, you will already be working toward achieving high rankings in all search engines.

We have spent quite a bit of time outlining a very basic marketing plan. There are several other references out there which I highly recommend you consider, as they will simplify the process and potentially save you hundreds of hours. They are:

- *How to Write a Great Business Plan for Your Small Business in 60 Minutes or Less* by Sharon Fullen and Dianna Podmoroff Item # GBP-01 $39.95

- *2,001 Innovative Ways to Save Your Company Thousands by Reducing Costs: A Complete Guide to Creative Cost Cutting and Boosting Profits* by Cheryl L. Russell Item # IWS-02 $21.95

- *How to Get the Financing for Your New Small Business: Innovative Solutions from the Experts Who Do It Every Day — With CD-ROM* by Sharon Fullen Item # HGF-01 $39.95

- *Getting Clients and Keeping Clients for Your Service Business: A 30-Day Step-By-Step Plan for Building Your Business* Item #GCK-01 $24.95

- *The Complete Guide to Working for Yourself: Everything the Self-Employed Need to Know about Taxes, Recordkeeping, and Other Laws —With CD-ROM* Item #WFY-01 $29.95

There are many other innovative and informative books published by Atlantic Publishing Company, which, in addition to the ones listed above, are available from their Web site at **www.atlantic-pub.com**.

Your online marketing plan does not need to be overly complex and should not be a time consuming process; however, it is important to map out your objectives, budget, and critical success factors so you can measure and evaluate your success in achieving them.

4

HOW TO GENERATE WEB SITE TRAFFIC WITH AND WITHOUT GOOGLE

Google is king in the search engine world, and your goal should be to obtain the highest site rankings possible. We will discuss search engine optimization (SEO) at length later in this book and how this will dramatically affect your overall site rankings; however, there are many other things you can do as an online business owner to generate Web site traffic. Web site traffic is the number of visitors and visits a Web site receives. This is determined by the number of visitors and the number of pages they visit. Web sites monitor the incoming and outgoing traffic to see which pages of their site are popular and if there are any apparent trends, such as one specific page being viewed mostly by people in a particular country. Most quality Web hosting companies provide you with detailed statistical analysis and monitoring tools as part of a basic hosting package.

Your Web site traffic can be analyzed by viewing the statistics found in the Web server log file or using Web site traffic analysis programs. A hit is generated when any file is served. The page itself is considered a file, but images are also files; thus, a page with five images could generate six hits (the five images and the page itself). A page view is generated when a visitor requests any page within the Web site — a visitor will always generate at least one page view (the home or main page) but could generate many more. There are many ways that you can increase your Web site traffic — all leading to greater sales and profit potentials. We will discuss a variety of options that will lead to increased Web site traffic.

HOW TO CREATE MEDIA EXPOSURE AND DRIVE CUSTOMERS TO YOUR WEB SITE

In this chapter we will explore how to generate Web site traffic by using Google and other sources of traffic which must be generated outside of Google or offline. Media exposure is a key component in your successful marketing profile and strategy. Your customers will form their opinions (positive or negative) based on what they hear and see in print, on television, on the radio, or on the Web. Recognizing the importance of media exposure and dedicating resources to promoting your online business can boost the sales of your products or services. That positive media exposure is also a major step toward maintaining credibility in your online marketplace and ensuring that you compel visitors to channel more traffic to your Web site — ultimately increasing volume and revenue.

The first thing you need to keep in mind is that media exposure, as with online marketing campaigns, which we will discuss in later chapters, will take some time to become effective. It is not going to happen overnight, and you will have to take the time to think about the direction in which you want that exposure to take you. Developing a tactical approach to media exposure should be part of your business objectives and marketing plan.

There are several things that you can do to promote your offline media exposure. These may include the following.

- Approach your local chamber of commerce and request that they write a short article about you and your business; even if you are an online-only business, the local exposure is great. You can then take that article and publish it on your Web site as another promotion tool or use it in an online e-zine campaign. (Refer to my book *The Complete Guide to E-mail Marketing: How to Create Successful, Spam-Free Campaigns to Reach Your Target Audience and Increase Sales* for more details on developing e-mail campaigns, as they are not part of this book.) You will want to make sure that the focus of the article is just as much about you as it is about the business you are promoting. Remember that you want to promote yourself as well as your business. The best local media exposure results if you are being viewed as a leader in your community.

- Offer to be a speaker at a seminar or lead a workshop in your area of expertise. This is a great way to gain media exposure that is incredibly positive and community oriented, thus giving you credibility and trust among potential clients. Circulate your URL and business information at the seminar. Put your Web site URL on everything you distribute (flyers, promotional items, business cards, letterhead).

- Follow up any correspondence or phone calls from the media with a letter or phone call. Make sure to leave your Web site URL on their voice mail. This strategy gains you media exposure by building a reputation as a conscientious, courteous entrepreneur.

- Share your knowledge by writing articles and professional

opinions for online publications and upload them to automated, e-zine syndication sites. These syndication sites are perfect for having immediate hotlinks back to your Web site and other specific landing pages. Remember to include your e-mail or your picture in the byline, as well as brief biographical information on yourself and your business. The more exposure you generate, the more successful your business will become. Give permission to authors to use your articles in their books, magazine, or publications, and be sure to require them to include a corporate biography and contact information in exchange for the permission.

- Develop tactics to make media exposure and coverage work for you. Make media friends wherever and whenever the opportunity presents itself. You are going to have to earn media exposure, but the time and effort that you expend will be worth it.

- Keep in mind that most columnists will give their e-mail address in their byline. Send them a note with your comments and views, while offering your expertise and establishing yourself as a source for future quotes. Optimize your media exposure whenever possible; the returns for your business will be substantial.

Media exposure can also be defined as "promotion and publicity" for the online success of your company. You need to make the media work for you, not against you, so that customers can easily find you, learn to trust you and your product, and keep coming back to your Web site for repeat sales. Your potential and existing customers are only going to buy products and services from a business that they feel is trustworthy. To earn that trust and reliance, you have to make the most of media exposure so that you can build your credibility and find a secure position for your business as an expert in your target market. What is going to work best is a combination of effective online and offline publicity and public relations that is geared toward affirming your corporate trustworthiness, reliability, and credibility.

Many businesses pay thousands of dollars for media exposure, publicity, and advertising. You can get free publicity and PR for your business's Web site by using proven methods that will garner media exposure. Many businesses pay upward of $5,000 or $10,000 for advertising. Your company can get that same advertising exposure with little to no money. By engaging in Internet media campaigns, or "non-traditional" media methods (such as pay-per-click marketing), for gaining media exposure, you can accomplish two things:

- Save a significant amount of money

- Be in full control of your own media techniques

Your customers are going to form negative or positive opinions about your business based on what they see and hear on the radio, on the television, or in print. Mass media, such as radio, television, and print, are often difficult and certainly costly methods to promote your business, so we will concentrate on less costly methods. By using positive media relations, you will be making enormous strides toward successful search engine positioning. This will allow you to convert more of your Web site traffic into satisfied and online success.

GAINING THE TRUST OF CLIENTS

Gaining the trust of your customers is extremely critical in developing a continuing relationship that rewards your online business with repeat customer sales. The one-time sale may boost your immediate sales numbers, but it is returning customers that take your business from mediocre profits to fantastic profits. Your goal is to build quality customer relationships and then maintain them. Gaining media exposure, both online and offline, opens the doors to a potentially long-term relationship with customers by using implied third-party credibility. Once you attract the prospects, you still have to deliver your goods/services and ensure that the customer is completely satisfied. One of the major advantages of using Google marketing tools is that the Google name is already equated with "trust." Google's reputation is superior, and you can leverage that reputation and trust in your marketing campaigns.

INCREASING YOUR PUBLIC PROFILE

The more positive your public profile, the more success you will have online and offline. This, of course, ties back in with gaining credibility with the public. Your public profile is your trademark for success and profits. Just as important, your online profile and business rating is critically important to how customers perceive you. Your local and state Better Business Bureaus are great organizations to join so you can obtain positive ratings. Other online business profile ratings services worth considering are **www.resellerratings.com**, **www.epinions.com**, and **www.consumerreports.org**. Do not underestimate the impact of a review of your business and/or products and services. You must ensure 100 percent customer satisfaction in service and product quality to make sure you gain only positive reviews for you and your company.

You want to establish a successful, upbeat profile that is based on your confidence and credibility supported by your products, services, and superior customer service and satisfaction. You can increase your public profile by taking advantage of opportunities that allow you to use your services and knowledge in a variety of venues, thereby gaining public awareness and online marketing exposure without spending your own funds on relatively expensive advertising. Think outside the box. Do not always stick to convention just because the business market dictates certain protocol.

Positioning yourself, and actually becoming an expert in your market, takes time, patience, and personal confidence. Knowing the advantages of effective marketing is half the battle. Remember that it is the combination of media and marketing that really communicates the benefits and unique aspects of your business, which in turn drive customers to your Web site. When you establish yourself as an expert in your market, others will be drawn to you for advice, sponsorship, professional opinion, and branding — all of which will have dramatic, positive impacts on your online business.

Your goal when it comes to sharing your expertise is to publish for free, thereby allowing many organizations, news services, and other publications or magazines to distribute your article throughout their distribution network in return for links back to your Web site and direct product promotions to thousands of potential new customers. There are ways that you can publish a full-page ad promoting yourself and your business without spending a dime. Contact editors and offer them your press release to add content to their next publication. Many editors are looking for useful and relevant content so that they can meet deadlines. You need to take advantage of this opportunity and create the perfect article for publication. Remember to always ensure that you require a corporate biography and full contact information to be published with your articles.

You should target newspapers, magazines, newsletters, Web sites, and Web magazines as ideal opportunities for displaying your article. Keep in mind that magazines that have an offline and an online image are excellent for increased exposure. Atlantic Publishing has produced e-zine newsletters for more than six years and has grown a significant subscriber database. They routinely publish articles at no cost to professionals within the industry, providing a variety of hyperlinks, company and product descriptions, and other promotional material all at no cost, driving thousands of potential customers to their Web site. There are many other companies desperately seeking contributions to their online newsletters.

WEB SITE ESSENTIALS

We discussed an online marketing strategy in the previous chapter, and this will refine your conversion of that strategy into real-time results. For your online strategy to be effective, you must have a Web site that is effectively designed and meets the needs of your site visitors. A poorly designed Web site, or one that is not functionally efficient, will drive away customers quickly. Make sure that your Web site is professional and has a great design. Professional site design means having a Web site that is

- Easy to navigate

- Has appropriate logos

- Has up-to-date information

- Answers customer questions

- Does not look like an amateur site

- Implements a sound search engine optimization plan

Never hide anything from your customers. Give them all the data they need to make an informative decision about your product or service. Follow through on what you say you offer at your Web site to maintain credibility and trust. You do not want to be identified and exposed in the media as a poor company, as a scam site, or as a con artist. Bad news travels fast, and it travels even faster on the Internet — quickly making your pay-per-click marketing campaign (or any other marketing campaign) a money loser.

USING PRESS RELEASES TO GENERATE WEB SITE TRAFFIC

We have already discussed the importance of media exposure. But what about using an online press release to get that same exposure to your customers? An online press release is part of the online medium of communication, and online communication is all about timing. Your press release, whether printed, faxed, or online, is one method of communicating with your customers and your industry.

Most companies use press releases to alert the public about a new product or a new service they offer. These press releases, while informative, tend to be somewhat dry, and consumers often skim over them, sometimes even missing the key points. If it is not newsworthy, you will not be selected for coverage. That said, a press release promoting specific events, specials, or newsworthy items can be very effective. The Silvermine Tavern (**www.silverminetavern.com**) has used effective press releases for years by publishing written press releases, which are printed in the newspaper, as has Atlantic Publishing Company through their press release web page (**http://atlantic-pub.com/pressreleases.htm**), which promotes new releases to libraries, book stores, re-sellers, and individual customers.

Silvermine Tavern publishes press releases online and also disseminates highlights through their online newsletter promotional program, gaining maximum promotional potential at virtually no cost. As an alternative to a written press release, you could try a multimedia approach. If you are giving a live press release, you can incorporate the audio or video files onto your Web site, either to complement a written press release or replace it altogether. It is highly recommended that you have a media section on your

Web site to serve reporters, columnists, producers, and editors with your latest press release information. Many people find listening to an audio clip or, better yet, watching a video clip preferential to reading a written press release. There is so much written word on the Internet that trying another medium could be just the boost your company needs. You should also think of other Web site owners as another channel since everyone is looking for fresh content and expert advice.

Consider using an online press release service, such as **www.PRweb.com**, to generate successful media exposure for your online business. Keep in mind the value of using highly relevant keywords often within the content of your online press release to take advantage of the benefits of search engine optimization (SEO). Including live links in your online press release is another way for you to ensure increased media coverage. Linking to relevant Web sites increases the credibility and functionality of your online business.

Make sure that you give your customers a reason to visit your site, to spend time browsing it, to interact with it, and most important, to return to it. Offer incentives by showcasing featured products or promotions, and use creative and new Internet tools, such as video and audio, to create an interactive experience. You can also import video clips from promotional products, CDs/DVDs, or create your own video clips and add them to your Web site.

ESTABLISH A WEB SITE PRIVACY POLICY

Internet users are becoming more and more concerned with their privacy. You should establish a "privacy" Web page and let your visitors know exactly how you will be using the information you collect from them. This page should include the following:

- For what do you plan on using their information?

- Will their information be sold or shared with a third party?

- Why do you collect their e-mail address?

- Do you track their IP address?

- You should notify site visitors that you are not responsible for the privacy issues of any Web sites you may be linked to.

- Notify them that you have security measures in place to protect the misuse of their private or personal information.

- Provide site visitors with contact information in the event that they have any questions about your privacy statement.

ESTABLISH AN "ABOUT US" PAGE

An "about" page is an essential part of a professional Web site for a variety of reasons. One reason is that your potential customers may want to know exactly who you are, and second, it is a great opportunity to create a text-laden page for search engine visibility. An about page should include the following:

- A personal or professional biography

- Photograph of yourself or your business

- Description of you or your company

- Company objectives or mission statement

- Contact information, including your e-mail address

ESTABLISH A TESTIMONIALS PAGE

Another way to develop credibility and confidence among your potential customers is to include previous customer testimonials. You need to make sure your testimonials are supportable; therefore, include your customer's names and e-mail addresses for validation purposes.

Using customer testimonials is a great way to promote the quality and reliability of your Web site and, more important, promote your products or services. This is an amazingly effective tactic. Direct customer testimonials are the strongest and most effective sales assistance you can get. I highly recommend using audio and video testimonials, as well as printed quotes.

Remember that no matter how flashy or impressive your Web site may look, it is customer service, satisfaction, and reliability that keeps customers coming back.

ESTABLISH A MONEY-BACK GUARANTEE

Depending on the type of Web site you are operating, you may consider implementing a money-back guarantee to eliminate any potential risk to customers purchasing your products. By providing them with a solid, no-risk guarantee, you build confidence in your company and your products.

ESTABLISH A FEEDBACK PAGE

There are many reasons to incorporate a feedback page into your Web site. Potential customers will have questions about your products and services or may encounter problems with your Web site, and the feedback page is an easy way for them to contact you. Additionally, it allows you to collect data from the site visitor, such as name, e-mail address, or phone number. A timely response to feedback ensures customers that there is a "living" person on the other end of the Web site, and this personal service helps increase the likelihood they will continue to do business with you.

ESTABLISH A COPYRIGHT PAGE

You should always display your copyright information at the bottom of each page. You should include both the word "copyright" and the © symbol. Your copyright should look similar to this:

Copyright © 2007 Profit Strategies & Solutions, Inc.

PROVEN TECHNIQUES FOR GENERATING WEB SITE TRAFFIC

The following techniques may be employed to increase Web site traffic. These proven methods will increase your Web site traffic.

- Create a "What's New" or "New Products" page. Site visitors like to see what is new, trendy, or just released. Make it easy for them.

- Establish a promotion program. The sky is the limit for promotions. You can offer free products, trial samples, or discount coupons. Everyone loves a bargain, so give it to them.

- Establish a contest. Contents cost nothing to create, are simple to manage, and draw visitors back.

- Add content-relevant professional articles, news events, press releases, or other topics of interest on a daily basis to draw visitors back to your site.

- Establish a viral marketing campaign or embed viral marketing techniques into your current advertising programs or e-zines. Viral marketing is when you incorporate such things as a "forward to a friend" link within the advertisement. In theory, if many people forward to many more friends, it will spread like a virus (hence the name viral) and eventually go to many potential customers.

- Use signature files with all e-mail accounts. Signature files are basically business cards through e-mail, so why not send your business card to all your e-mail recipients? Signature files are sent with every e-mail you send out and can contain all contact information, including business name and Web site URL. Signature files can be created in Microsoft Outlook or Outlook Express.

- Start an affiliate program and market it. Include your affiliate information in e-mails, newsletters, e-zines, and on Web sites to promote your program. A successful affiliate program will generate a significant increase in Web site traffic. For an example of a highly effective affiliate campaign, visit: **http://www.atlantic-pub.com/affiliate.htm**.

- Include your Web site URL on everything (business cards, letterhead, promotional items, e-mails, and so on).

- Win some awards for your Web site. There are quite a few award sites which are nothing more than link exchange factories; however, there are some reputable award sites such as **www.webbyawards.com** and **www.100hot.com.**

- Everyone loves search engines, so put Google right on your Web site (more details on how to do this later). Simply visit Google to add a free search feature to your Web site. This is a great tool, which site visitors will love.

- Implement Google AdSense on your Web site to increase revenue and traffic.

- Implement Google AdWords to increase Web site traffic and generate sales revenue.

- Register multiple domain names with search engines and "point" them to your main Web site. Owning similar or content-related domain names is a good investment to protect yourself from competitors stealing similar-sounding domain names and will help you with search engine rankings.

- Put your URL into your e-mail signature so you are constantly advertising your Web site.

- Put your Web site URL on your business card.

- Register your site with online directories relevant to your content.

- Write free articles and submit them to other newsletters.

- Post often on content-related forums and message boards and post your Web site URL with each entry.

- Submit content often to content-relevant e-mail discussion groups and post your Web site URL with each entry.

- Establish links from other sites to yours (backlinks). Create a links page or directory on your site and offer your visitors a reciprocal link to your site for adding a link to yours on theirs.

- Create an exciting contest on your Web site to draw in traffic. Free items and exciting contests are extremely popular and are very appealing.

- Develop quality Web site content that is well-organized and captivating.

- Use eBay to generate Web site traffic by registering your eBay store with search engines.

- List your URL on all offline advertising and printed materials (i.e. stationary, print advertisements).

- Begin a business blog on your Web site. If it is well done and has relevant content, people will link to it, increasing your site's visibility and ranking in search engines.

As you may have figured out, this chapter is not exactly related to Google. The reason for this is that you must employ a wide variety of approaches in your marketing plan to drive customers to your Web site. The techniques I have listed are essential to generating Web site traffic. When implemented in conjunction with effective search engine optimization they will generate Web site traffic and increase your customer base and revenue.

5

INTRODUCTION TO PAY-PER-CLICK ADVERTISING

The key concept you need to understand about pay-per-click advertising is that, unlike other paid advertising campaigns where you pay for the campaign itself in hopes of generating customers and revenue, you are not paying for any guarantees or promises of sales, Web site traffic, or increased revenues. You are not paying for traditional advertising campaigns hoping for a 1 to 2 percent return on your investment, and you are not paying for placing a banner advertisement on a Web site and hoping that someone actually sees it, is interested, and clicks on it. Google makes pay-per-click advertising easy with Google AdWords, which we discuss in detail in the next chapter. Let us look at pay-per-click advertising.

Banner advertising was the largest type of advertising on the Internet, and it still holds a small market share; however, the main disadvantage of banner advertising is that the ads are embedded in pages, and you have to rely on Web designers to put your ad on a page that has similar or complementary content. A banner advertisement for dog food will likely not do well if it is placed on a Web site about computer repairs. Enter the beauty of pay-per-click advertising. You do not pay to have your advertisement loaded on a Web page, you do not pay to have your advertisement listed at the top of search engines, and you only pay for results. In other words, pay-per-click advertising is entirely no cost (minus potential setup costs), even if your advertisement is viewed by millions of Web site visitors.

You will only pay when someone actually "clicks" on your Google AdWords advertisement. When someone clicks on your AdWords advertisement, Google charges your account, based on a formula price, and the customer will be navigated to the page on your site that you have preset when you created your pay-per-click advertisement. Bear in mind that the "click" in no way guarantees you any sales; it merely means that someone has clicked on your advertisement. Do not underestimate the importance of having a user-friendly, information-rich Web site to capture the attention of the site visitor and close the deal. Not all pay-per-click campaigns must result in a purchase — many advertisers use pay-per-click advertising to sell products; however, many more use them to sell services, promotional material, news releases, and other media intended to build business or disseminate information.

Pay-per-click advertising was started in 1998 by a company called **Goto.com**, which eventually become **Overture.com** and was then purchased by Yahoo. The original concept was that anyone with a brick and mortar or online business could manage and determine their own search engine ranking based on pre-selected keywords and how much money they were willing to pay for the resulting "click" on their advertisement.

Pay-per-click advertising is the fastest growing form of online marketing today and the future only looks brighter and stronger. Pay-per-click advertising sales are expected to exceed $15 billion in 2007 and will continue to grow at a staggering 40 percent or more annually.

You, as an advertiser, Web site owner, or corporate manager will quickly admire the simplicity and functionality of pay-per-click advertising, which allows you to have significant control over your campaign. Before you forge the path towards implementing a pay-per-click marketing plan, it is critical to understand pay-per-click advertising and develop strategies to design an effective campaign, optimize and monitor overall ad performance, and employ sound business principles in the management and financial investment of your campaign. One of the success factors in creating and managing a pay-per-click campaign is the effective selection and use of keyword and advanced statistical reporting tools from Google and your Web hosting company. To ensure the potential for success of a pay-per-click campaign you must choose the most effective keywords, design an effective and captivating advertisement, and have a well-designed, information-rich Web site with easy navigation.

PAY-PER-CLICK ADVERTISING WALKTHROUGH

You, as the advertiser, pay a rate you specify for every visitor who clicks through from the search engine site to your Web site. Every keyword has a "bid" price, depending on the popularity of the keyword in search engines. You set your own budget and financial limitations, and you are done. Here is a step by step walkthrough:

- You, as the advertiser join Google AdWords and put money on your account to get started.

- You create your ad as you want it to appear with your own selected keywords.

- Based on the keyword value, you set how much you are willing to spend on each keyword. Obviously, the more popular keywords are more costly per click than others.

- Upon completion, your ad will appear in the Google search engine.

- When someone searches through Google, by using one of your keywords, the advertisement is matched to the keyword query and the ad is displayed in the results.

- If the person "clicks" on your advertisement, they are navigated to your Web site, and you are "charged" for the click.

The search engine will return a rank-ordered list of the most popular Web sites matching your search criteria, and it may display your advertisement if it also matches the search criteria and keyword. One of the benefits of Google AdWords is that your advertisement will be placed right up there with the top ranked Web sites in your search category.

Most pay-per-click search engine applications operate on the same principle and rule: The advertiser with the highest bid gets top billing in the search engine return. It is a combination of experience, knowledge of the market, and some trial and error that lets you balance keywords and phrases to deliver optimal results, and the tools provided by Google AdWords help you achieve that goal.

GOOGLE ADWORDS PAY-PER-CLICK BENEFITS

- Google AdWords pay-per-click advertising is instantaneous and easy to implement.

- Google AdWords pay-per-click advertising results are clearly measurable.

- Google AdWords pay-per-click advertising is cost effective in comparison to other types of traditional and online advertising programs.

- Google AdWords pay-per-click advertising is for large and small businesses.

- Google AdWords pay-per-click advertising is ideal for testing out market response to new products or services.

- Google AdWords pay-per-click advertising gives you full control over your budget — you can set systematic budgetary limits to minimize your overall financial risk and investment.

- Google AdWords pay-per-click advertising is more effective than banner advertising.

- Google AdWords pay-per-click advertising delivers a higher click through rate than banner advertising.

- Google AdWords pay-per-click advertising is ideally placed with top search engine results on the world's most popular search engine.

- Google AdWords pay-per-click advertising is only delivered to your potential customers when they are actually searching on keywords related to your products or services contained in your pay-per-click ad.

- Google AdWords pay-per-click advertising is delivered based on keyword searches and delivered immediately — meaning the chances of turning one of those potential customers into an actual customer is dramatically increased.

- Google AdWords pay-per-click advertising allows you to design your ad, which is strategically placed in a prominent location on the Web site, instead of flashy, annoying banner advertisements that turn off potential customers.

- Google AdWords pay-per-click advertising can be delivered in search engine results (which is the most common) or they can be delivered in the content of a Web page.

Throughout this book we will use Profit Strategies & Solutions, Inc. as one of our case studies. Profit Strategies and Solutions is a nationally recognized, independent food service profit strategies firm dedicated to the successful conceptualization and implementation of maximizing the profits of food service companies. Located in Lake Oswego, Oregon, their team of restaurant consultants, restaurant accountants, and food service experts help their clients realize their maximum profit potential. Using ChefTec recipe software and restaurant consulting services, the company works to increase the profitability of restaurant businesses because they understand the unique challenges and pitfalls associated with the hospitality industry. The use of this software saves the end user from initially entering and creating databases for food and alcohol recipe and inventory control.

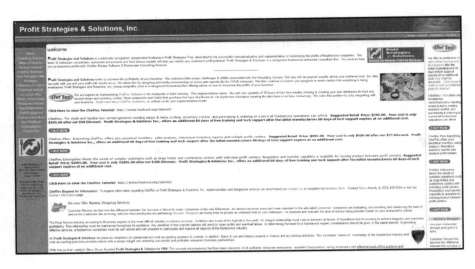

We performed a search on Google looking for "ChefTec." A screen shot of the results is below. The top eight rankings in Google are listed along with "sponsored links" on the right hand side of the screen. You will notice the number one sponsored search ad is from Profit Strategies and Solutions (**www.restaurantprofits.com**). This is an example of a pay-per-click advertisement.

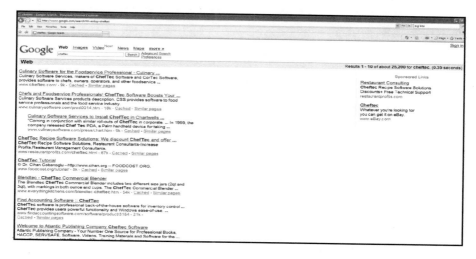

Screenshots (C) Google Inc. and are reproduced with permission.

If I were to click on this advertisement, Profit Strategies and Solutions would be charged a fee for this "click."

Screenshots (C) Google Inc. and are reproduced with permission.

You should also notice that Profit Strategies & Solutions is the #4 ranked company in the Google search engine rankings (the top 3 are the manufacturer of ChefTec Software), and the #8 ranked company is Atlantic Publishing Company (**www.atlantic-pub.com**).

ChefTec Recipe Software Solutions: We discount **ChefTec** and offer ...
ChefTec Recipe Software Solutions, Restaurant Consultants-Increase Profits,Restaurant Management Consultants.
www.restaurantprofits.com/cheftec.html - 67k - Cached - Similar pages

ChefTec Tutorial
© Dr. Cihan Cobanoglu --http://www.cihan.org -- FOODCOST.ORG.
www.foodcost.org/tutorial/ - 5k - Cached - Similar pages

Blendtec - **ChefTec** Commercial Blender
The Blendtec ChefTec Commercial Blender includes two different size jars (2qt and 3qt), with markings in both ounce and cups. The ChefTec Commercial Blender ...
www.everythingkitchens.com/blendtec-cheftec.htm - 54k - Cached - Similar pages

Find Accounting Software :: **ChefTec**
ChefTec software is professional back-of-the-house software for inventory control ... ChefTec provides users powerful functionality and Windows ease-of-use. ...
www.findaccountingsoftware.com/software/product/3154 - 21k - Cached - Similar pages

Welcome to Atlantic Publishing Company **Cheftec** Software
Atlantic Publishing Company - Your Number One Source for Professional Books, HACCP, SERVSAFE, Software, Videos, Training Materials and Software for the ...
www.atlantic-pub.com/cheftec.htm - 37k - Cached - Similar pages

Screenshots (C) Google Inc. and are reproduced with permission.

When I click on the pay-per-click advertisement for Profit Strategies & Solutions, I am navigated to their Web page, which promotes the sale of ChefTec Solutions software. Also, when I click on the link in the search results for Profit Strategies & Solutions, I am brought directly to the Web page that promotes the sale of ChefTec Solutions software. Of course, Profit Strategies & Solutions is not charged for this click since this is not a paid advertising listing. It is worth noting that the link for Atlantic Publishing Company also returns a link directly to the ChefTec sales page on their site, which normally means that both sites are effectively managing search engine optimization to ensure maximum visibility with relevant links in major search engines.

Another primary benefit of a pay-per-click campaign is that you have fully customizable advertising solutions. You can literally create dozens of separate pay-per-click ads, with different wording and based on different keywords, all in a single advertising campaign. This gives you tremendous flexibility to target a wide array of potential customer segments. Having a wide variety of advertisements available is a critical component of pay-per-click marketing.

COST OF PAY-PER-CLICK ADVERTISING

Pay-per-click advertising is, of course, limited by the size of your advertising budget. You will know in advance how much you will pay per click, and most start out with a minimum price per click, such as $0.10 and can quickly escalate to significantly more, even as much as $100 per click, depending on the keyword.

The concept is fairly simple. Let us say you want to sell a particular product by utilizing a pay-per-click advertising campaign. For the sake of this example, let us say we are selling Atlantic Publishing Company's award-winning book *The Restaurant Manager's Handbook*, and I decided to use the keyword phrase "restaurant management" in our Google AdWords pay-per-click advertisement. Restaurant management is a fairly common topic, and there are many others who want to use restaurant management as the keyword phrase in their pay-per-click ad, and all of us want to be the top ranked listing. Essentially, we "bid" against our competitors with the amount we are willing to pay for each click. It may be cost prohibitive to be the top bidder, as your advertising budget will be consumed much quicker than if you were a #2 or #3 bidder; however, there are also times when it is more critical to be the number one bidder, regardless of the financial impact. Your bid is the maximum amount you are willing to pay for the Web site visitor to click on your advertisement, so be careful when bidding. We will discuss bidding in detail later in this book.

In the next couple of chapters we will concentrate on creating Google AdWords specifically.

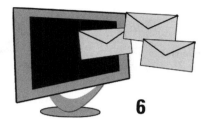

6

USING GOOGLE ADWORDS

Google is the most popular search engine in the world today, and it also boasts the number one pay-per-click advertising program: Google AdWords. Throughout this chapter I will provide you with a detailed guide to Google AdWords. The concept behind Google AdWords is very simple. Google states that, with Google AdWords, you perform three simple steps, which you can also find online (**http://adwords.google. com/select/Login**):

- **Creation of Ads** — You first must craft your advertisements and decide on your keywords. These are the words that you feel specifically relate to your business.

- **Appearance of Ads** — When someone performs a search with one of your keywords, your ad will appear on the right side of the screen. This ensures that your ad is being viewed by people who are already interested in your product or service.

- **Attraction of Customers** — If someone clicks on your ad, he or she can buy your product or service. Google will even make a page for you, free of charge.

Google AdWords provides you with:

- **Targeted Reach** — AdWords allows you to target new audiences based on specific keywords.

- **Greater Control** — You have the flexibility to revise your ad and your budget until you get the desired results. Additionally, you are able to create a variety of ads and direct them at a specific demographic.

- **Measurable Value** — There is no contract, which means that you do not have to spend a certain amount of money or dedicate a certain amount of time to your campaign. You are only charged when someone clicks on your ad, which helps bring you potential customers.

WHAT IS GOOGLE ADWORDS?

Google AdWords is user-friendly, and is a quick and simple way to purchase highly targeted cost-per-click (CPC) or cost-per-impression (CPM) advertising. AdWords ads are shown along with search results on Google, as well as on search and content sites in Google's ever growing network. These sites include AOL, EarthLink, HowStuffWorks, and Blogger. When you create an AdWords keyword-targeted ad (pay-per-click advertisement), you choose keywords for which your ad will appear and specify the maximum amount you are willing to pay for each click. You will only pay when and if someone clicks on your ad. Google AdWords also features the AdWords Discounter, which automatically reduces the actual CPC you pay to the lowest cost needed to maintain your ad's position on the results page.

When you create your AdWords site-targeted ad, you choose the exact Google Network content sites where your ad will run and specify the maximum amount you are willing to pay for each thousand page views on that site. You pay whenever someone views your ad, whether the viewer clicks or not. We recommend you start out with Google AdWords keyword targeted ads and do not allow content-matching. There is no minimum monthly charge with Google AdWords; however, there is a one time activation fee for your account. Although your campaign can literally start in minutes, we highly recommend you invest the time to identify the best keywords possible and follow our guidance on creating your ad.

WHERE WILL MY GOOGLE ADWORDS ADVERTISEMENT APPEAR?

Your Google AdWords advertisement could appear on all the search and content sites and products in the Google Network. The Google global search network includes Google Base (the old Froogle), Google Groups, and the following:

Screenshots (C) Google Inc. and are reproduced with permission.

Google's AdWords Content network of high-quality consumer and industry-specific Web sites and products includes:

Screenshots (C) Google Inc. and are reproduced with permission.

HOW ARE GOOGLE ADWORDS RANKED?

The maximum cost-per-click (CPC) and the ad's Google quality score are how keyword-targeted ads are ranked on the results page from a search (**Ad Rank = CPC x Quality Score).** Google determines the quality score by that keyword's performance history on Google, as well as its click-through rate (CTR), the relevance of the ad's text, the landing page quality, among other relevancy factors.

Google states that having relevant keywords and ad text, a strong click-through rate on Google, and a high cost-per-click will result in a higher position for your pay-per-click advertisement. One of the main advantages of this system is that you cannot be locked out of the top position as you would be in a ranking system based solely on price.

For a keyword-targeted ad's position on a content page, Google's system considers two things:

- The ad group's content bid or, if content bids are not enabled, its maximum CPC

- The ad's past performance on this and similar sites

When you have completed the account setup process, you will be required to activate your account through an opt-in e-mail. When this is confirmed, your account is activated and you can log into your new Google AdWords account. At this point you will be required to enter your billing information. When this is done, your ad typically appears within minutes. Google AdWords is set up to operate with three distinct levels: Account, Campaign, and Ad Group. The list below shows the account structure and the settings that are applied at each level. You can also visit **http://www.google.com/ ads/aw_faq.html** for more information. In summary:

- Your account is given its own e-mail address, password, and billing information.

- If your account is on the Campaign level, you have the ability to choose your budget, target market, and start and end dates.

- If your account is on the Ad Group level, you have the ability to create your ads and specify your keywords. In addition, you can choose the maximum cost-per-click you are willing to pay for each keyword.

- In your Ad Group, you can choose which keywords will trigger which ads. There is a specific set of keywords assigned to each Ad Group.

- You can view your ads' click through rates, giving you the power to remove or edit any underperforming ads.

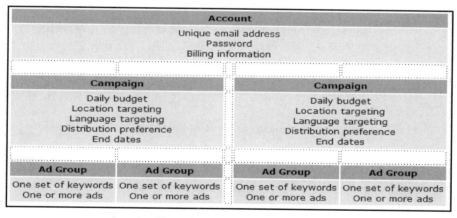

Screenshots (C) Google Inc. and are reproduced with permission.

HOW MUCH WILL GOOGLE ADWORDS COST?

You will pay a $5 fee to set up your Google AdWords account. Each keyword has a minimum bid based on the quality of the keyword specific to your account. If your keyword or Ad Group's maximum cost-per-click (CPC) meets the minimum bid, your keyword will be active and trigger ads. If it does not, your keyword will be inactive for searches and not trigger ads on

Google or its partner search sites. Remember to use the tips we provided regarding how to successfully bid on keywords. When you review your account, your keywords will be listed as "active" (which will trigger PPC advertisements) or "inactive" (which will not trigger PPC advertisements). Some key cost factors to remember:

- The position of an ad is based on the maximum CPC and quality.

- The higher the quality score, the lower the CPC required to trigger ads, and vice versa.

- There is no minimum spending requirement.

- The activation fee is a one-time $5 charge.

- You set the daily limit on how much you are willing to spend.

- You set how much you are willing to pay per click or per impression.

- You only pay for clicks on your keyword-targeted advertisement.

- You only pay for impressions on your site-targeted AdWords advertisement. We recommend you start out with keyword targeted ads until your campaign is well established.

ESTABLISHING AND MANAGING YOUR GOOGLE ACCOUNT

Google provides a wide variety of tools to help you establish your account, choose keywords, manage your budget, and manage your account in detail. The Google Keyword Tool generates potential keywords for your PPC campaign and tells you their Google statistics, including search performance and seasonal trends. You simply enter potential keyword phrases or a specific URL, which will generate suggested keywords for you based on the Web site content. You can then add new keywords to your campaign. The following screen shot depicts the Keyword tool:

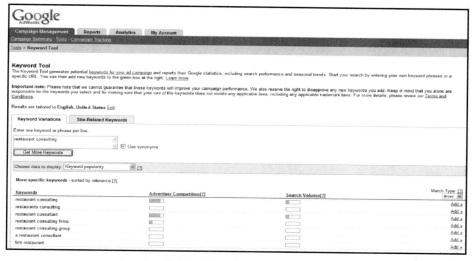

Screenshots (C) Google Inc. and are reproduced with permission.

The screen shot below depicts the Site-Related tool. Remember, if you are targeting products or a certain page on your Web site, enter that URL to generate keywords, instead of your home page:

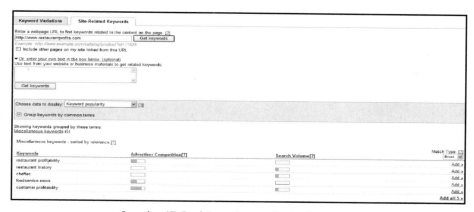

Screenshots (C) Google Inc. and are reproduced with permission.

You may wish to incorporate Negative Keywords into your campaign. Negative keywords prevent your ads from appearing for queries containing the negative keyword. Google offers a tool that simplifies the process of creating negative keywords and incorporating them into your campaign. A screen shot of the Negative Keyword tool is below:

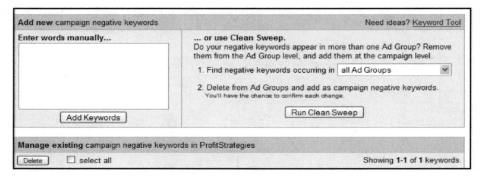

Screenshots (C) Google Inc. and are reproduced with permission.

THE GOOGLE TRAFFIC ESTIMATOR

The Google Traffic estimator tool provides a wealth of data relevant to your chosen keywords and helps you determine expected traffic, daily budget, costs per keyword, and campaign success. Remember, this is simply a tool. It is not a guarantee of performance; however, it is based on the best data in Google and should be representative of what you may expect. See a screenshot of this tool on the following page.

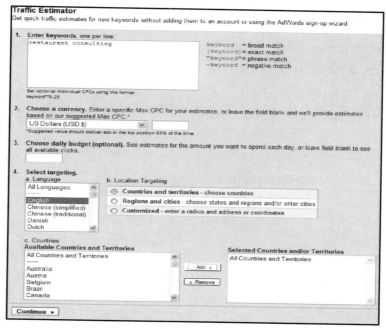

Screenshots (C) Google Inc. and are reproduced with permission.

You simply enter keywords into the appropriate fields, along with some optional entries, such as maximum cost per click, daily budget limits, as well as targeted languages and locations, and click "continue" to see the results. The results provide you with an average cost per click, volume, estimated ad position, estimated number of clicks per day, and estimated cost per day.

Average CPC: **$8.19** (at a maximum CPC of $17.32)
Estimated clicks per day: **17 - 20** (at a daily budget of $150.00)

Estimates are based on your bid amount and geographical targeting selections. Because the Traffic Estimator does not consider your daily budget, your ad may receive fewer clicks than estimated.

Maximum CPC:	Daily budget:	Get New Estimates				
Keywords ▾		Search Volume	Estimated Avg. CPC	Estimated Ad Positions	Estimated Clicks / Day	Estimated Cost / Day
Search Total			$6.54 - $9.87	1 - 3	17 - 20	$80 - $150
chaflec			$0.71 - $0.89	1 - 3	0	$1
recipe software			$10.06 - $15.09	1 - 3	1	$6 - $20
restaurant consulting			$1.69 - $2.53	1 - 3	6	$10 - $20
restaurant management			$5.93 - $8.90	1 - 3	10 - 13	$70 - $120

Estimates for these keywords are based on clickthrough rates for current advertisers. Some of the keywords above are subject to review by Google and may not trigger your ads until they are approved. Please note that your traffic estimates assume your keywords are approved.

Screenshots (C) Google Inc. and are reproduced with permission.

GOOGLE ADWORDS CAMPAIGN SETUP

The first step you must complete is to create a new Google AdWords campaign. Remember that you can have many campaigns in one Google AdWords account. To create a new campaign, click on the Create a New Campaign Link on the Google AdWords Campaign Management Screen.

All Campaigns

+ Create a new campaign : keyword-targeted

Screenshots (C) Google Inc. and are reproduced with permission.

You may choose keyword-targeted (target customers by keywords) or site-targeted (target customers by Web sites). We recommend you choose keyword-targeted. Keyword-targeted campaigns will appear on Google's results page whereas site-targeted will appear on Web sites that you have selected in the Google network. You must name your campaign; choose a name that will help you easily and quickly identify which campaign it is. This is important if you create multiple campaigns in your account.

You will also have to choose the Ad Group name. The Ad Group name contains one or more ads that target one set of keywords or sites. You will set your maximum cost per click or cost per thousand impressions (CPM) for all the keywords or sites in the Ad Group. You may also set prices for individual keywords or sites within the Ad Group. Again, if you are setting up a keyword-targeted campaign, you need to set up the maximum cost-per-click for the keywords, not the sites, which are used for site-targeted campaigns. Additionally, you will choose the targeted customers by language and location.

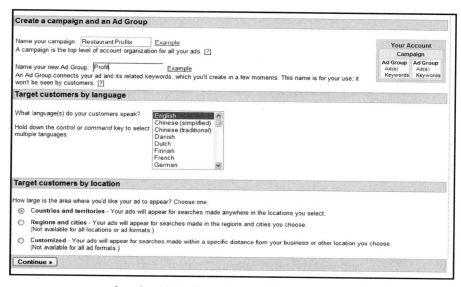

Screenshots (C) Google Inc. and are reproduced with permission.

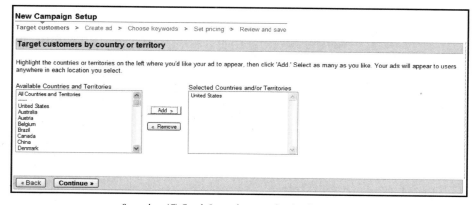

Screenshots (C) Google Inc. and are reproduced with permission.

Next you will create the actual advertisement that will be displayed in the search engine results page. Google AdWords has multiple ad options, including:

- Text Ad:

Luxury Cruise to Mars
Visit the Red Planet in style.
Low-gravity fun for everyone!
www.example.com

Screenshots (C) Google Inc. and are reproduced with permission.

81

- Image Ad

Screenshots (C) Google Inc. and are reproduced with permission.

IMAGE SIZE SPECIFICATIONS (IN PIXELS)	
468 x 60 Banner	300 x 250 Inline
726 x 90 Leaderboard	336 x 280 Large Rectangle
200 x 200 Small Square	120 x 600 Skyscraper
250 x 250 Square	160 x 600 Wide Skyscraper

- **Local Business Ad** — Local business ads are AdWords ads associated with a specific Google Maps business listing. They appear on Google Maps with an enhanced location marker. They also show in a text-only format on Google and other sites in the search network.

- **Mobile Text Ad** — Your ads will appear when someone uses Google Mobile Search on a mobile device.

Screenshots (C) Google Inc. and are reproduced with permission.

- Video Ad — Video advertisements are a new format that appears on the Google content network. Your video ad will appear as a static image until a user clicks on it and your video is played.

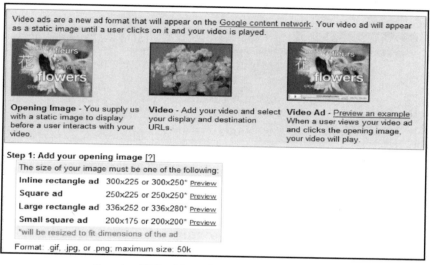

Screenshots (C) Google Inc. and are reproduced with permission.

We recommend your start out your campaigns with the text advertisement. Google AdWords provides you with a simple form to create your text advertisement. As you enter data, the example is updated with your data.

You will need to give some extra time and attention toward the wording of your advertisement. Wording can be tricky because of the limited space you are given, as well as the restrictions imposed by Google. Google AdWords has a clear policy on how to create the advertisement.

On the following page you will find an advertisement for a fictitious business we created to help you create ads called Gizmo Auto Sales, **www. gizmoautosales.com**. You may not be able to use superlatives such as finest, best, biggest, nor are they recommended. You are also restricted from promotional punctuation, such as the ! and $ symbols. You are limited on the number of words capitalized, and you cannot use all caps.

THIS AD WILL NOT PASS REVIEW

Lowest Used Auto Price Quotes — Get them NOW!

Save $$CASH$$ with Discount Prices

www.gizomoautosales.com

THIS AD WILL PASS REVIEW

Used Automobile Price Quotes — Free all the Time

Save money with Discount Auto Prices

www.gizmoautosales.com

It is critical to load the title (first line of your PPC ad) with keywords. PPC programs may have different rules that apply in regards to the title line; however, you should strive to load it with keywords, while maintaining readability and strive to make it captivating to a potential customer. Your goal is simply to capture the attention and interest of a potential customer. If you can do that, your ad is successful. If no one is interested in your advertisement, it will not get clicks and will not draw customers to your Web site. Test multiple versions of the advertisement to see which works best and change keywords to help you analyze which is most effective. Review the ads of competitors; you may find they are outperforming you simply because their advertisement is better written, more captivating, or has more customer appeal.

The use of the words free, rebate, bonus, and cash are perfect to attracting the attention of Web site surfers. Other words which may encourage Web site visitors to click through your advertisement should be used, as long as your message is concise and clear. Do not overload them with words that take away from the meaning of your advertisement. Remember that Google must review and approve your advertisement, and if your ad does not pass their review, you will notified.

You should also consider the domain name listed in your advertisement, as it may have an effect on your ability to draw in potential customers. Your domain name should be directly related to your product or services and be professional in nature. The domain name reallycheapcars.com may not impart a perception of quality in your automobiles that you are striving to achieve. Perhaps the domain name qualitycars.com would be a better choice. Also, be wary of domain names that are overly promotional in content, as these may drive away potential customers (i.e., freecars.com).

You will find an abundance of companies which offer search engine copywriting services, which is a good option if you are having problems developing successful advertisement campaigns.

Some recommended sources for copywriting include:

- http://www.searchenginewriting.com/

- http://www.grantasticdesigns.com/copywriting.html

- http://www.roncastle.com/web_copywriting.htm

- http://www.futurenettechnologies.com/creative-copy writing.htm

- http://www.tinawrites.com/

- http://www.brandidentityguru.com/optimized-copy writing.html

Search engine copywriting is critical to a successful PPC advertising campaign. While we have recommended professional services for this task, it is not overly difficult to achieve if you apply some basic discipline and rules. While I have repeatedly stressed the insertion of keywords into an advertisement, simply cramming keyword after keyword into your PPC ads may be counter-productive and doing so is not search engine copywriting. Successful search engine optimization copywriting takes planning, discipline, analysis, and some degree of trial and error.

The following are some general guidelines for successful search engine optimization copywriting:

- **Use no more than four keywords per ad.** Four keywords provide a wide variety without saturating the ad with keywords and losing the meaning of the ad.

- **Use all your allowed characters in each line of the advertisement.** The length depends on the PPC provider; however, use the space you have been provided. There is no incentive for white space.

- **Write in natural language where possible.** "Natural language" is a popular term used extensively with copywriting. It simply means that the reader should not be able to detect the keywords the advertisement is targeting. The best advertisements are written for an individual to read and understand, embedded with subtle keywords, and projecting a clear message so that it reads naturally. The opposite of this is a keyword-crammed advertisement that is nothing more than a collection of keywords and is entirely un-natural to read.

- **Use keywords in the title and description lines.** However, use common sense and follow the rules we provided so that you do not overload them with keywords.

- **Test and tweak.** Test your advertisement and analyze your reports and results. Your advertisement may need tweaking and improvements, or it may be entirely ineffective and may need to be replaced.

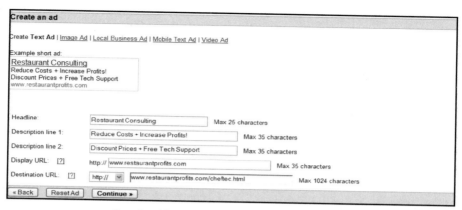

Screenshots (C) Google Inc. and are reproduced with permission.

Google will check your advertisement and Web site for content, functionality, and to ensure the ad complies with editorial guidelines.

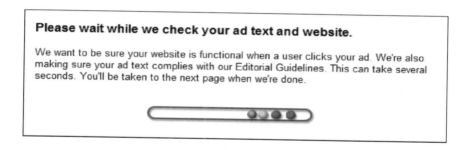

Screenshots (C) Google Inc. and are reproduced with permission.

Google AdWords will extract keywords from your site based on a scan of the Web site URL and propose them to you as potential keywords to use on your campaign. You may choose any keywords suggested or enter any of your own into the campaign window. Google recommends a maximum of 20 keywords per advertisement for best results. After you have selected keywords that closely match your products or services, click the "continue" button.

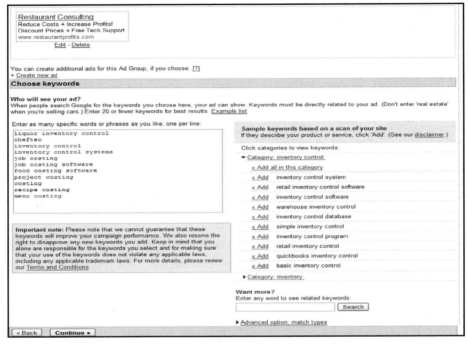

Screenshots (C) Google Inc. and are reproduced with permission.

You must now enter your budgetary constraints and limitations, such as the daily budget. When the daily limit is reached, your ad will stop showing for that day. The budget controls the frequency of your ad, not its position. You may raise or lower your budget amount as often as you like. Additionally, you must choose your maximum cost per click, which is the highest price you are willing to pay each time a user clicks on your advertisement. Your maximum CPC can be changed as often as you desire.

What is the most you would like to spend, on average, per day?

The daily budget [?] controls your costs. When the daily limit is reached, on average, your ad will stop showing for that day. (The budget controls the frequency of your ad, not its position.) Raise or lower your budget as often as you like.

Enter your daily budget: $ [   ]

What is the maximum you are willing to pay each time someone clicks on your ad?

You influence your ad's position by setting its maximum cost per click (CPC) [?]. The max CPC is the highest price you're willing to pay each time a user clicks on your ad. Your max CPC can be changed as often as you like.

Enter your maximum CPC: $ [   ] (Minimum: $0.01)
Higher CPCs lead to higher ad positions, which usually get more clicks.

Want to purchase the most clicks possible?

▸ View Traffic Estimator - Enter a CPC and see the estimated rank, traffic, and costs for your keyword(s).

Three things to remember:

- You can always change your CPC and budget, or pause your account entirely.
- Your budget controls your spending. If your daily budget is $5.00 and there are 30 days in a month, you'll never be charged more than $150 in that month.
- Lower your costs by choosing more specific keywords, like *red roses* instead of *flowers*. Specific keywords are more likely to turn a click into a customer. Edit your keyword list.

[« Back] [Continue »]

Screenshots (C) Google Inc. and are reproduced with permission.

You may discover that the costs can escalate quickly without setting daily and monthly budget limitations. Keep in mind that limits on your daily/ monthly budgets will also affect your ad performance because your ad will not be displayed after you hit your budget limits. Google recognizes when your advertisement is bumping against it budget constraints and may suggest you increase your budget amount to increase visibility of your advertisement:

💡 **Campaign Budget Alert**
In the last 15 days, your ads missed 46% of impressions for which they were eligible. Increasing your budget could allow your ads to show more often and get more clicks.
Tell me more | Remove this message

Screenshots (C) Google Inc. and are reproduced with permission.

THE GOOGLE CAMPAIGN SUMMARY

The Campaign Summary screen is where you will control all your Google AdWords campaigns. At this screen you will be presented with an overview of each campaign, including campaign name, status, budget, clicks, impressions, click through ratio, average cost per click, and total cost. Note that the data is presented based on the reporting period selected.

All Campaigns + Create a new campaign : keyword-targeted	site-targeted [?]		Aug 1, 2006 to Aug 31, 2006 last month					
Pause Resume Delete Edit Settings Show all but deleted campaigns								Go
☐ Campaign Name	Current Status	Current Budget [?]	Clicks	Impr.	CTR	Avg. CPC	Cost
☐ ProfitStrategies	Active	$5.00 / day	194	17,727	1.09%	$0.77	$149.70
Total - 1 all but deleted campaigns	-	$5.00 / day active campaigns	194	17,727	1.09%	$0.77	$149.70
Total - all 2 campaigns	-	$5.00 / day active campaigns	194	17,727	1.09%	$0.77	$149.70

Screenshots (C) Google Inc. and are reproduced with permission.

To drill down into each campaign, simply click on the campaign name to view a detailed status based on keywords and ad variation performance. This module will help you determine the effectiveness of each keyword, as well as add or remove keywords. Your keywords may be marked "inactive for search" in the "status" column and stop showing on search results if they do not have a high enough quality score and maximum cost-per-click (CPC). This is another way of saying that your keyword or Ad Group's maximum CPC does not meet the minimum bid required to trigger ads on Google or its search network partners. This normally occurs when keywords are not as targeted as they could be, and the ads they deliver are not relevant enough to what a user is searching for, which ultimately means you need to refine your keywords or your advertisement.

Keywords marked inactive for search are inactive *only* for search. They may continue to trigger ads for content sites if you have the Google content network enabled for that campaign. Again, we recommend that you turn off this feature initially and only use keyword searches because a keyword marked as inactive for search may continue to generate clicks and charges on the content network. If your keyword is inactive for search, you may increase your keyword's quality score by optimizing for relevancy. Optimization is a technique for improving the quality of your keywords, ad, and campaign to increase your keyword's performance without raising costs. Try to combine your keyword with two to three other words to create a more specific keyword phrase. This will result in better targeting and potentially better performance. You may also Increase your keyword's maximum cost per click to the recommended minimum bid. Your keyword's minimum bid is the amount required to trigger ads on Google and is determined by your keyword's quality score. When your maximum CPC falls below the minimum bid, your keyword will be inactive for search. For this reason, you can simply increase your maximum CPC to the minimum bid to re-activate your keywords. You may also choose to delete all your keywords that are inactive for search.

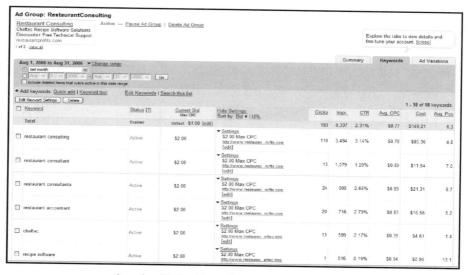

Screenshots (C) Google Inc. and are reproduced with permission.

The Ad Variations link allows you to review the performance of each advertisement within a selected campaign. It is common to have multiple ads created for the same or different keyword combinations in the same campaign. In the example on the next page, it is clear by the percent served that the first advertisement is served considerably more than the second advertisement, which is rarely served. The reasons for this may vary, depending on the keywords chosen or the campaign settings.

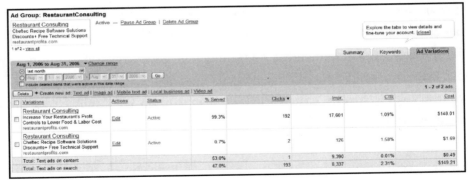

Screenshots (C) Google Inc. and are reproduced with permission.

If you click on the Edit link, under the Actions column, you can tweak your campaign advertisements to improve your statistics.

Screenshots (C) Google Inc. and are reproduced with permission.

Remember, for each Ad Group you create, you can create up to 50 ad variations. The variations can be in any of the formats offered for AdWords, including text, image, and video ads. When you first sign up for an account, you will be offered the chance to create additional ad variations immediately after you create your first ad. You can also create ad variations later, after your account is running. Sign into your account and choose the Ad Group you want to work with. Click the Ad Variations tab, find the line reading "Create new ad," and then select the type of ad you want to create. All ad variations in a single Ad Group are triggered by the same set of keywords. You can choose to have ads optimized automatically, so that the best-performing ad variations show most often, or you can choose to show them evenly regardless of their performance. You may choose to have ads optimized to show better-performing ads more often (and is the default selection) or rotate, which shows all ads equally. If you want different ads to appear for different keywords, you can create multiple Ad Groups or campaigns.

The Edit Keyword Settings page helps you track individual keywords and their costs. You may enter individual maximum cost-per-click or destination URLs for any keyword.

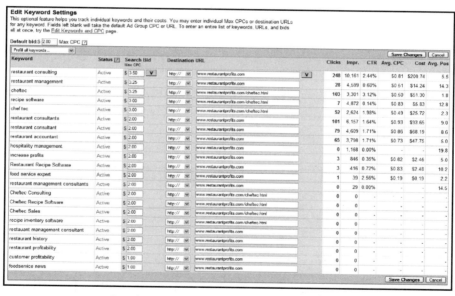

Screenshots (C) Google Inc. and are reproduced with permission.

EDITING YOUR CAMPAIGN SETTINGS

In the "Edit Campaign Settings" menu, you have the ability to modify your campaign settings, including campaign name, budget options, ad scheduling, keyword bidding, networks (which specify keyword search or content search), target audience, and ad serving (which allows you to optimize the ads or rotate them evenly).

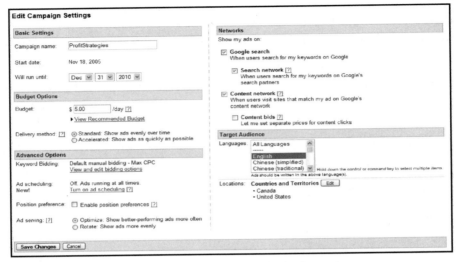

Screenshots (C) Google Inc. and are reproduced with permission.

Google AdWords will suggest the recommended budget amount for your campaign by clicking on the View Recommended Budget link in the Edit Campaign Settings screen.

Based on your current keywords, your recommended budget is $8.00 / day.

If the recommended amount is too high, try raising your budget to a comfortable amount. Or, to make the most of your budget, try refining your ads and keywords.

Screenshots (C) Google Inc. and are reproduced with permission.

Ad scheduling lets you control the days and times your AdWords campaigns appear. Your AdWords ads normally are available to run 24 hours a day. Ad scheduling allows you to set your campaigns to appear only during certain hours or days of each week. For example, you might set your ads to run only on Tuesdays or from 3 until 6 p.m. daily. With ad scheduling, a campaign can run all day, every day, or as little as 15 minutes per week.

To determine when you want your ads to show, you may want to run an hourly report. Ad scheduling can be used with both keyword-targeted and site-targeted AdWords campaigns. If you select the advanced setting, the bid multiplier will apply to both cost-per-click (CPC) and cost-per-thousand-impressions (CPM) bids. Ad scheduling will not raise or lower your budget. The AdWords system will try to reach your usual daily budget in whatever number of hours your ad runs each day.

Position preference lets you tell Google where you would prefer your ad to show among all the AdWords ads on a given page. Whenever you run a keyword-targeted ad, your ad is assigned a position (or rank) based on your cost-per-click (CPC) bid, your keyword's quality score, and other relevant factors. There may be dozens of positions available for a given keyword, spread over several pages of search results. If you find that your ad gets the best results when it is ranked, for example, third or fourth among all AdWords ads, you can set a position preference for those spots. AdWords will then try to show your ad whenever it is ranked third or fourth and avoid showing it when it is ranked higher or lower. If your ad is ranked higher than third for a given keyword, the system will automatically try to lower your bid to place your ad in your preferred position.

You can request that your ad be shown only when it is:

- Higher than a given position, such as above seven

- Lower than a given position, such as below four

- Within a range of positions, such as from two to eight

- In a single exact position, such as position two

Position preference does not mean that your ad will always appear in the position you specify. The usual AdWords ranking and relevance rules apply. If your ad does not qualify for position number one, setting a position preference of one will not move it there. Position preference simply means

AdWords will try to show your ad whenever it is ranked in your preferred position and to avoid showing it when it is not. Position preference also does not affect the placement of AdWords ad units on the left, right, top, or bottom of a given page. It only affects your ranking relative to other ads across those units.

Google AdWords allows you to track conversions. In online advertising, a conversion occurs when a click on your ad leads directly to user behavior you deem valuable, such as a purchase, sign up, page view, or lead. Google has developed a tool to measure these conversions and help you identify how effective your AdWords ads and keywords are. It works by placing a cookie on a user's computer when he or she clicks on one of your AdWords ads. Then, if the user reaches one of your conversion pages, the cookie is connected to your Web page. When a match is made, Google records a successful conversion for you. Please note that the cookie Google adds to a user's computer when he/she clicks on an ad expires in 30 days. This measure, and the fact that Google uses separate servers for conversion tracking and search results, protects the user's privacy. You may select Conversion Tracking under your campaign main menu, and there are some minimal setup requirements for Conversion Tracking to work.

GOOGLE ADWORDS REPORTS

Google provides full online statistical, conversion, and financial reporting for the Google AdWords program. You can view all your account reports online 24 hours a day, 7 days a week, and you can also have them set up to be e-mailed to you on a scheduled basis. You have a variety of advanced reports available, including:

- **Statistical Reporting:** Displays the average actual cost-per-click (CPC), the number of times your ads were shown (impressions), how many times users clicked on your ads (clicks), and your ad and keyword click through rates (CTR). This reporting is available for each of your keywords, ad variations (such as text ads, image ads, video ads, mobile ads, and local business ads), Ad Groups, campaigns, and account.

- **Financial Reporting:** Review a detailed billing summary and itemized payment details that include invoice dates, invoice numbers, specific and summary campaign costs, and billing adjustments.

- **Conversion Reporting:** Track your AdWords conversions (successful sales, leads, or submissions)

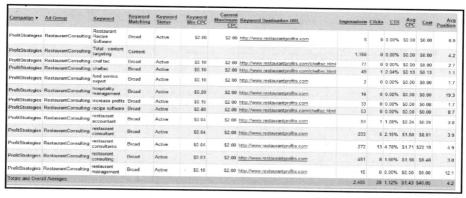

Screenshots (C) Google Inc. and are reproduced with permission.

GOOGLE ADWORDS SITE EXCLUSION

Site Exclusion allows you to specify Web sites by URL Web sites in Google's content network which you want to be excluded. Implementing this feature will prevent your ad from appearing on the sites you have specified.

GOOGLE ADWORDS ADS DIAGNOSTIC TOOL

One of the nicest features of Google AdWords is the Ads Diagnostic Tool, which helps you find out why your ads may not be showing on the first page of search results for a certain keyword. Let us look at our advertisements for **www.restaurantprofits.com**, specifically the ChefTec product:

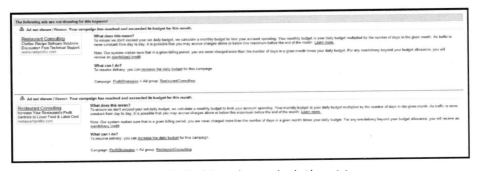

Screenshots (C) Google Inc. and are reproduced with permission.

When we search for the term "cheftec," we get some interesting results. In the results below we see that our advertisement campaign has reached its maximum budget and is no longer being served in search results. Google provides you with detailed instructions on how to increase the budget and resume delivery.

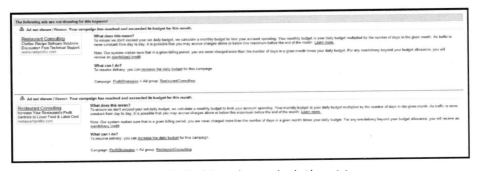

Screenshots (C) Google Inc. and are reproduced with permission.

Increasing your CPC to or above the minimum bid will help improve your keyword performance. However, the best way to ensure a high ad placement and top performing keyword is by optimizing your keyword, ad, and campaign for quality.

TIPS, TRICKS, AND SECRETS FOR GOOGLE ADWORDS PAY-PER-CLICK ADVERTISING

Here is a compilation of some tips and hints that will help you develop and manage a highly effective Google AdWords campaign, which in turn will generate higher click through rates, lower your cost per click, and get conversions (i.e., click throughs that result in a sale of your product).

- Design Google AdWords ads so they target potential customers who are ready to buy. Rarely will banner ads or pay-per-click ads draw in the curious Web site browser and result in a sale.

- Ensure your Google AdWords ad is very specific in nature.

- Target one product for each Google AdWords ad if possible, instead of a generic ad that targets a large market segment.

- Make your ad link directly to the product page, instead of a generic page or the Web site home page.

- If your Google AdWords ad targets a very specific product, you may see a reduction in actual clicks (because your advertising segment is narrow); however, those clicks are most likely extremely profitable since you are only getting clicks from individuals seeking information on your specific product. This means your advertising cost may actually be reduced, while your sales go up.

- Be willing to bid for a good position. If you do not want to spend much money and are willing to settle for the bottom of the bids, no one is going to see your ad.

- Bid enough to gain the exposure you need, but balance exposure to stretch your advertising budget. It is often not worth the cost to have the number one bid, and it is often significantly less costly if you are in positions two through ten.

- Being the number one listing on search engines may not be all it is cracked up to be. The top listing is the one that is clicked most often, but also has the worst percentage of converting clicks into actual sales. Many "click happy" people click on the top listing without ever converting a sale. Those "clicks" will quickly eat up your advertising budget. You may have better luck by being below the number one listing since the potential for better qualified clicks exists as potential customers screen all the advertisements, instead of just clicking on the first one.

- Use the provided tracking tools to monitor performance and adjust keywords/bidding as necessary.

- Choose very specific keyword phrases. You will lower your overall costs while increasing the potential conversion rate by choosing multiple, highly targeted words (or phrases) instead of generic terms in an attempt to get tons of traffic. For example, use "Crystal River Florida Vacation Rental Home" instead of "Florida Rental."

- Use capital letters for each word in the title and in the description fields of your ad.

- Use demographic targeting with your Google AdWords ad. If your intended audience is in the United States, there is no sense in allowing your PPC ad to be viewed elsewhere.

- Use Google AdWords Ad Targeting if you are trying to target a specific geographic area, such as the Washington, D.C. area.

- Use the Google Keyword Suggestion Tool to help you determine which keywords are most effective for your campaign.

- Keep an eye out for fraud. Google has fraud detection and prevention, but if you suspect your competition is clicking on your ads you may want to invest in additional protection such as **www.whosclickingwho.com/.**

- Check the spelling in your Google AdWords ad to ensure it is correct.

- Embed keywords in your actual Google AdWords PPC ad. This may help them stand out among competitor ads when scanned by potential customers.

- Define your target audience and narrow the scope of your advertisement to potential customer markets. If you do not sell overseas or in foreign speaking countries, do not pay to have your advertisement listed there.

- Develop multiple advertisements for each campaign and run them at the same time. You will quickly determine which is effective and which is not. Do not be afraid to tweak advertisements or replace poor-performing advertisements.

- Monitor and utilize Google Reports by tracking your costs, return on investment (we showed you how to calculate that earlier), and the click through ratios for each advertisement. Implement Google Conversion Tracking to track the effectiveness of completing a sale.

- Include Targeted Keywords in the headline and description lines of your advertisement. Keywords stand out in search engine results and help to attract the attention of potential customers, as well as increase your advertisement effectiveness.

- Make your advertisement stand out by announcing what your company product does that others do not. For example, in addition to selling ChefTec Software, Profit Strategies & Solutions, Inc. offers 60 days of free training and tech support after the manufacturer's 60 days of tech support at no additional cost.

- Do include words which stand out and grab the attention of potential customers, such as free, new, limited offer, and the like.

- Free may not be good for you. If your advertisement says "free," you can expect lots of traffic by folks who just want the free stuff and will never buy anything. This will just increase your costs. Consider limiting the use of free offers to cut back on traffic that will never culminate in a sale.

PRACTICAL ADVICE FOR MANAGING YOUR GOOGLE ADWORDS ACCOUNT

- Google provides you with Conversion Tracking and we highly recommend taking the time to install it.

- Monitor your daily and monthly budget on a regular basis. This is even more important if your campaign becomes successful because it will cost more. Most companies set daily and monthly limits and forget about the budget. As your desire to get the top page listings increases, so does your tendency to "bump" up the budget a few dollars a day or add another $1.00 per click. Before you know it your campaign costs can double or triple.

- Monitor your daily and monthly budget and number of clicks. You may find your ads will no longer be served for a majority of each month if you hit your daily and monthly limits early in the month. It is not uncommon for new AdWords customers to set a monthly limit of $100 per month. It is also not uncommon for the $100 to be used within the first week, meaning your ads are not served for the remaining three weeks of the month. The same applies for daily limits — a low daily limit may minimize the number of hours your ad may be displayed.

- Use multiple marketing schemes, including Google AdWords, AdSense, and other Google applications.

- Google AdWords allows you to test multiple ads based on the same keyword group and do it simultaneously. By creating different advertisements you can track each individually and determine which is the most effective. When you determine which are less effective, you can tweak them and change the wording to improve their success.

- Be realistic in your expectations. Although your Google AdWords pay-per-click campaign can be established quickly, do not expect your business to quadruple the first day you campaign is established. It takes time, patience, and constant monitoring and modification for your campaign to become highly effective.

- Spend the time to research your keywords and develop quality keywords. Believe it or not, the time spent will result in less cost and better quality click through rates. Your conversion rates will improve dramatically with highly relevant, targeted, and refined keyword lists.

- There are plenty of free resources on the Internet about how to effectively manage your AdWords campaigns. Use them. The advice of experts is valuable when creating and managing your accounts. Become active in pay-per-click discussion forums to exchange ideas and experiences with AdWord, and you will acquire more tips and tricks to improve your campaigns.

- Create your advertisement with relevant and targeted keywords and ad copy. Type "used car" into the Google search engine and you will get 13,000,000 links and tons of advertisements. However, this is such a broad category you may never find the used car you are looking for. Now type in "porsche 911" and you get 1,100 links and lots of advertisements, but the advertisements are much more targeted and relevant. By creating relevant and targeted advertisements, you can eliminate many clicks. Your goal is to keep costs low by eliminating unnecessary clicks.

- There is no magic bullet, secret formula, or hidden code to rocket you to success. It takes time, attention, work, and more work. Eventually, if you follow the principles in this book, you will see increased Web site traffic, a growing customer base, and conversions from your Google AdWords campaign.

A great source to read is an article titled *Guide to Google AdWords — Target Your AdWords Ads for Motivated Visitors* by Peter Bergdahl (**http://www. articlealley.com/article_92745_6.html**).

HOW TO CHOOSE EFFECTIVE KEYWORDS & KEY PHRASES

Web site traffic is the amount of visitors and visits a Web site receives. As we have discussed in detail, more than 80 percent of Web site traffic originates from a search engine, and Google is the search engine leader. It is vitally important that you implement search engine optimization techniques to raise the visibility and ranking of your Web site in search engines and pay-per-click advertising campaigns. It is important to determine what keywords or key phrases your potential customers may use when seeking out your company, products, or services.

A keyword is a word or phrase that people (consumers or businesses) employ to locate information on the products, services, or topics. When choosing the keywords you will eventually bid on and embed in your advertising campaign, you need to think like a potential customer, not as the seller or advertiser. You must determine which search terms a potential customer might use to find you through search engines. Getting high rankings in a search engine and high visibility of your PPC ad based on keywords is directly related to how competitive the keyword is. Remember, you do not own any keywords, and chances are your competitors are targeting the exact same keywords; therefore, you will find the cost to buy a keyword in a Google PPC advertising campaign is primarily determined by how many other Web sites are competing for the same keyword or key phrases.

The formula for determining the cost of a keyword varies by PPC companies; however, the primary factor in determining cost is the relationship of the keyword to top ten rankings in a search engine. If your keywords are not competitive (in other words, not many companies are trying to use the same keywords in their campaign), the cost of the keyword is relatively low and will yield high search engine rankings.

If you are competing with hundreds of thousands of other companies for the same keywords, the cost of those keywords will escalate dramatically as each company strives to outbid the others in the fight to claim one of the top positions — often highly contentious keywords can cost up to $100 each per click, quickly consuming advertising budgets. Google AdWords minimum cost-per-click base rates depend on your location and currency settings. Your minimum cost-per-click (CPC) rates can fluctuate for each keyword based on its relevance or quality score. The quality is the most important factor in determining the cost you will pay when someone clicks on your ad. Your quality score, which is determined by your keyword's click-through rate, relevance of ad text, historical keyword performance, and other relevancy factors, sets the minimum bid you will need to pay for your keyword to trigger ads. If your maximum CPC is less than the minimum bid assigned to your keyword, you will need to either raise the CPC to the minimum bid listed or optimize your campaign for quality.

Source: **www.google.com**

It is important that you understand how the process works so you can determine in advance which keywords are most effective and most cost efficient. Remember that the higher the quality score, the lower the minimum bid and cost you will pay when someone clicks on your ad.

Therefore, the best way to drive your advertising costs down is to maintain high-quality keywords, ads, and campaigns. Content clicks may be priced differently than search clicks in Google AdWords. Using smart pricing, Google can automatically adjust the cost of clicks for ads that appear on content network pages. While you set one maximum CPC, if Google data shows that a click from a content page is less likely to turn into actionable business results, such as online sales, registrations, phone calls, or newsletter signups, Google will reduce the price you pay for that click.

For example, let us assume you are running an AdWords ad for digital cameras. One of our content partner sites displays your ad. The first page of the site is an article about photography tips; the second page offers digital camera reviews. Because digital camera reviews is more product-specific than photography tips, a user who clicks your ad on this page is more likely to make a purchase than a user who clicks your ad on the photography tips page. In this example, Google will reduce the price of the click on the photography tips page because the estimated value is lower.

Source: **www.google.com**

A key principle in selecting keywords is determining how often someone will actually search the Web using that keyword or key phrase. Keywords that are less competitive typically bring you less traffic simply because the keyword is not used often during a search. Conversely, you can expect more traffic with highly competitive keywords; however, this may not always be the case as the field of competitors grows directly in proportion to the keyword competitiveness. When you begin your PPC campaign, you should be provided with in-depth analyses on a regular basis to help you monitor, adjust, and evaluate the performance of your marketing campaign. These reports should tell you exactly what keywords are being used by people who are using search engines with your campaign and helps you determine if your chosen keywords are effective.

GOOGLE ADWORDS COMMON TERMS

Keyword — These are the words you choose to market your ads to your potential customers.

Campaign — One or more Ad Groups is referred to as a campaign. Ad Groups share the same budget, language and country targeting, end dates, and distribution options.

Ad Group — A group of one or more ads that target a specific set of keywords. You can set your maximum price for an entire group or for specific keywords.

Impression (Impr.) — This term refers to the number of times an ad is displayed.

Keyword Matching Options — The four types of keyword matching (broad, exact, phrase, and negative) can help you refine your targeting methods.

Maximum Cost-per-Click (CPC) — You can decide how much you want to pay when your ad is clicked.

Maximum Cost-per-Impression (CPM) — You can decide how much you want to pay for every one thousand impressions.

Source: **www.aldenhosting.com/tips/Make_Money_Fast_With_Google_Adwords.shtml**

KEYWORD RESEARCH TOOLS

Another method to determine your keywords is to use one of the many keyword research tools provided on the Internet. Please note that not all these tools are free. Some of the keyword research tools are:

- WordTracker (**www.wordtracker.com**) — Promises to find the best keywords for your Web site. I entered "restaurant consulting" into the generation tool, and the application returned the following list of generated keyword suggestions:

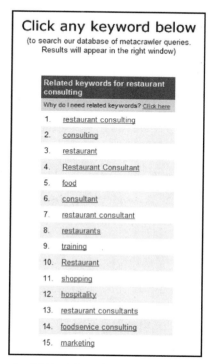

Screenshots (C) Google Inc. and are reproduced with permission.

You choose the keywords you want to use and the application returns "count" and "prediction reports." Count is the number of times a particular keyword has appeared in the WordTracker database, while prediction is the maximum total predicted traffic for all the major search engines/pay per bids and directories today.

Click here to add all keywords to your basket			
Keyword (?)	Count (?)	Predict (?)	Dig (?)
restaurant consulting	36	47	✎
restaurant consulting memberships	10	13	✎
restaurant consulting deer	6	8	✎
restaurant consulting - newbie clubs	5	6	✎
consulting management restaurant	3	4	✎
san francisco restaurant consulting	3	4	✎
free business consulting in the restaurant busine	2	3	✎
free business consulting in the restaurant busine	2	3	✎
restaurant consulting - start-ups	2	3	✎
restaurant consulting jobs	2	3	✎

Screenshots (C) Google Inc. and are reproduced with permission.

- Google **(https://adwords.google.com/select/KeywordTool External)** — The Google Keyword Tool generates potential keywords for your ad campaign and reports their Google statistics, including search performance and seasonal trends.

Screenshots (C) Google Inc. and are reproduced with permission.

The Google Keyword Tool can generate a variety of data, including keywords, keyword popularity, cost and ad position estimates, global search positive trends, and negative keywords. Of the tools listed, Google is by far the most user friendly and comprehensive. There are also dozens of other keyword generation tools available on the Internet.

Screenshots (C) Google Inc. and are reproduced with permission.

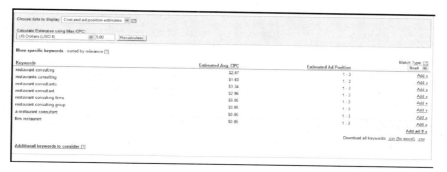

Screenshots (C) Google Inc. and are reproduced with permission.

The detailed reports provided from your PPC provider track each search term that resulted in somebody clicking on your advertisement. By analyzing this report, you can determine which keywords are effective and which are not. Since you can modify keywords at any time, it is well worth the analysis on your performance reports to understand how your ad is doing.

HOW TO DEVELOP KEYWORDS

One of the biggest challenges when establishing your Google AdWords PPC campaign is developing your initial list of keywords and key phrases. We have shown you how to perform research with your list of keywords; however, you must have a list of "potential" keywords or key phrases to start that process in the first place. Here are some hints and tips on how to develop your initial keywords and key phrases:

- Brainstorm and develop a list of all the possible keywords or key phrases you believe people might try to find your Web site.

- Screen your employees, friends, and customer base for a list of all the possible keywords or key phrases they would use.

- Screen your competitors' Web sites for a list of all the possible keywords or key phrases on their Web site.

- Take your entire list of keywords and key phrases and use the tools we have provided to refine your list and identify the most competitive and cost-effective keywords.

IN-DEPTH COMPETITIVE ANALYSIS AND KEYWORD RESEARCH TOOLS

By Carsten Cumbrowski

Introduction

Keyword research is the single most important task related to all of the following: SEO (search engine optimization), organic search engine optimization for existing pages, and also paid search and pay-per-click marketing campaigns.

Along with keyword research, another critical component of marketing is competitive intelligence. Knowing what your competition is doing will help you to make strategic decisions. Online marketers have a distinct advantage over their offline peers: They can access valuable information about their competitors' marketing activities. When you do your homework, you can learn a lot about what your competitors are doing — how much they are spending for specific marketing campaigns; their campaign targets; and the type of business optimization strategies they are employing.

Competitor Analysis: Tools and Services

The campaigns to which I am referring are search marketing campaigns, which are among the most important mechanisms for building an online business. Data about your competitors' campaigns are accessible at various levels of accuracy and detail on the Internet. Offline, competitive intelligence analysts might have to break laws to get this type of information. But online, this information is readily (and legally) available if you know where to look!

IN-DEPTH COMPETITIVE ANALYSIS AND KEYWORD RESEARCH TOOLS

There are a number of tools and services that can help you with competitor analysis. The data provided by any service or tool are always estimates, never exact figures. Relying on the data for exact figures is a mistake. Before you make important decisions, use alternate services and then compare what you find. Most importantly, be informed about which sources are used by each service or research tool.

Well known competitive intelligence tools and services and keyword research tools include Trellian's Competitive Intelligence, HitWise, Wordtracker, Keyword Discovery, the Overture Bid and Keyword Tools and WordZe.

With exception of Overture, services and tools are available only to paid subscribers. Fees can range from $20 to $50 per month up to thousands of dollars per month.

SpyFu

There is a free tool that offers almost as many features as those well known paid services. It's been flying below the radar for a while.

The name of the tool is SpyFu. Provided by VelocityScape, SpyFu is the sequel to the popular and free tool GoogSpy and can be found at SpyFu.com. If you know about GoogSpy, you will be amazed to experience the improvements of SpyFu.

SpyFu offers free Web site and keyword analysis for organic and paid searches. It has more than 20 times the amount of data than its predecessor, GoogSpy, and tons of other features.

You can approach the data from three angles, and change the approach instantly because SpyFu provides cross links for any detail shown in its result pages. The three angles are:

- Keyword or key phrase research and analysis
- Web site (domain) data including top keywords and top competitors
- Category-specific data

1. Keyword-specific data

SpyFu lets you see information like average cost per click for a specific keyword, clicks per day, number of advertisers, cost per day, and search results in Google. You can also see which sites compete for the keyword in the organic and paid search results. It also reveals other keywords used by your competition, as well as related keywords.

Let's try an example. If you own a Web site that sells bonsai trees and you would like to get a sense of what your competitors are doing, go to SpyFu.com, set up a

IN-DEPTH COMPETITIVE ANALYSIS AND KEYWORD RESEARCH TOOLS

free account, and enter the keyword "bonsai." First you'll see the AdWords results: a list of your competitors (and, I hope, your site!) and how much each pays per click for the keyword "bonsai." Next, you'll see organic search results — that is, the sites that come up "at the top of the list" when the term "bonsai" is entered into one of the search engines.

You'll be able to review a list of ad terms that your competitors have purchased (in this case the list includes misspellings of the term "bonsai").

2. Web site-specific data

Click on the name of each Web site to get even more information — like the site's average number of clicks per day, the number of incoming links, load time, etc.

SpyFu also shows known sub-domains and in some cases even allows drilldowns to individual pages. You can see the top organic and top paid search competitors and the Web site category/niche to which each was assigned based on its ranking and advertising behavior.

In the case of our example, you can learn a lot about sites that are paying 40 cents per click for the term "bonsai" — including other terms for which they are paying considerably less.

3. Category-specific data

SpyFu shows per category additional subcategories, related search terms, and related domains. In the case of our example, we learn that the search term "bonsai plant" is much more expensive than "bonsai." We can also see related domains and their top organic and ad competitors.

Conclusion

SpyFu provides a lot of information and is unusually comprehensive for a free tool.

The only drawback of SpyFu is that the beta version does not provide current data. The information on the free beta site is a few months old. Because of that, you should use it only as a guide, to get an overall idea what your competitors are doing and to find keyword ideas that you might want to explore. Use it in conjunction with other tools and services if you want to find out how accurate the provided numbers are.

This tool is a cost-effective resource that should not be missing from the bookmark list of any serious Internet marketer.

IN-DEPTH COMPETITIVE ANALYSIS AND KEYWORD RESEARCH TOOLS

For the big players out there who are looking for a smart investment: VelocityScape could be worth some due diligence as the next competitive intelligence solution.

*Carsten Cumbrowski runs the Internet marketing and Web development resources portal Cumbrowski.com (**www.cumbrowski.com**). He has years of experience in affiliate marketing and knows both sides of the business; the affiliate side since the beginning of 2001 and the advertiser/merchant side since 2002.*

His work in affiliate marketing also got Carsten involved in marketing methods like PPC search and search engine optimization among other methods and activities. Carsten was born in Berlin/East Germany and moved to the United States in May 2000. He is currently living in Fresno/California.

He is a blogger at ReveNews.com, a blogger community with over 20 professionals of the affiliate marketing industry contributing to it.

ReveNews was voted "Best Affiliate Marketing Blog" in 2006 by the readers of MarketingSherpa. He is also an editor and contributor at the search marketing news blog SearchEngineJournal.com.

©2006-2007 Carsten Cumbrowski. Reprinted with Permission

Keywords are the building blocks of your successful PPC advertising campaign. If you do not invest the time and research to choose the best possible keywords for your campaign, your campaign will suffer. Keep in mind that the more specific your keyword or key phrase is, the more likely a potential customer who may be looking for your products or services will find them. Careful and repetitive analysis of your keywords is the secret formula for PPC search engine success. While the time investment is significant, so are the results of refining and improving your keyword effectiveness — ultimately you will be rewarded in revenue sales.

An article that may be of assistance is "The Importance of Keyword Marketing for Newbies" by Richard East. This article provides insight into keyword marketing for both PPC and search engine optimization for your Web site. It is broken into two parts and is available at **http://www.**

THE COMPLETE GUIDE TO GOOGLE ADVERTISING

articlealley.com/article_56070_62.html and **http://www.articlealley.com/article_55978_81.html**.

TIPS AND TRICKS WHEN DEVELOPING KEYWORDS OR KEY PHRASES

The following is a compilation of the tips, tricks, and best practices that you can employ to assist you in the process of creating your keywords and key phrases for your PPC campaign.

- Brainstorm a list of any relevant keywords or key phrases you can think of. Take some time away from the list and over a period of seven to ten days keep adding more potential keywords and key phrases. It is not uncommon to have thousands of keywords initially for your campaign.

- Be sure to incorporate your company name, catch phrases, slogans, or other recognizable marketing material into keywords.

- Add both the singular and the plural spellings for your keywords.

- Add your domain names to your list of keywords. You will be surprised how many people search for a company by the URL instead of the company name (i.e., atlantic-pub.com instead of Atlantic Publishing Company).

- Take a peek at the meta tags on competitors' Web sites, in particular the "keywords" tag. Review this list and add them to your keywords list.

- Avoid trademark issues and disputes. Although there is some degree of latitude in regard to trademarks, my recommendation is to avoid using other companies' trademarks unless you are an authorized distributor or reseller of their products.

- Put keywords in the title of your PPC advertisement to generate a much higher click-through rate.

- Use bold face font in the title of the PPC ad.

- Find your target audience.

- Incorporate words that add to your PPC ad, such as amazing, authentic, fascinating, powerful, revolutionary, unconditional, and so forth.

- End your ads with words that promote an action on the part of the reader, such as "Be the First," "Click Here for All the Details," "Limited Time Offer," or "Free Today."

HOW TO ESTABLISH A BUDGET FOR YOUR PAY-PER-CLICK CAMPAIGN

Google AdWords PPC advertising allows you to quickly pay to have your ad listed on Google and Google partners. Since they are considered "sponsored links," they are significantly different than standard search engine results. These links will ultimately affect your advertising budget as you must pay for each "click." Sponsored links, or PPC ads, often appear at the top, bottom, or right side of the results page following a search with any search engine.

You may see Google AdWords advertisements called Sponsored Links. PPC advertising allows you to have your ad listed on search engines with the agreement that you will pay for each "click" on your advertisement based on bids you have placed on your chosen keywords. When your advertisement is clicked, depending on the keyword used to perform the search and the value of that keyword, you pay a fee to Google for that click.

We have discussed that the relative position or placement with search engine results are based on the keyword bidding system in which you directly compete with competitors to determine the value of the keyword and your relevant placement in the search engine results as determined by your maximum cost-per-click. It is important to note that there are additional factors, depending on the search engine, that will determine your actual ad placement beyond just the cost per keyword. Google uses a formula to calculate your PPC ad's position, which is calculated by multiplying your bid amount by your ad's click-through rate. It is not uncommon that ads with a higher click-through rate may appear higher in the "sponsored listings" than other ads with a higher bid amount.

Google requires you to pay per click based on pre-negotiated costs per keyword. PPC campaigns are set up with a credit card, and you must pre-load funds into your account. Since you have no control over who will click on your ad or how often, you are taking a financial risk based on the keyword costs times the number of clicks on your PPC ad. You do have some significant control over your budget since you can:

- Establish a Maximum Cost-per-Click

- Establish a Maximum Daily Total

- Establish a Maximum Monthly Total

You will need to make a decision about how to launch your campaign. Your choices are:

- **Exact Match** — The most precise matching that requires an exact match of all keywords. This is a good program since you only have highly qualified results, and there is less impact on your budget. We recommend you start with Exact Match PPC.

- **Content Match** — A less restrictive matching. If the person searching includes additional words before or after the keyword phrase, or if the general "content" of your keyword phrases are a close match, your ad will be displayed. We do not recommend you implement a Content Match campaign until your campaign is refined and tested, and then only if your budget allows.

PAY-PER-CLICK BUDGET PLANNING

You need to determine a manageable budget before starting your PPC campaign. Establishing a monthly budget for your Google AdWords campaign is difficult because pricing is based on keyword bids, which change in value often, and go up in cost over time. Most businesses tend to shift advertising funding from traditional marketing programs (print media, radio) toward PPC advertising. An alternative method is to estimate your increased revenue based on your PPC campaign and establish a percentage-based budget (percent of anticipated or realized increased revenue due to the PPC campaign). The advantage here is that you can scale the percentage up or down based on actual sales derived from the campaign. Google provides you with a Budget Optimizer for AdWords, which helps you receive the highest number of clicks possible within your specified budget.

MEASURING RETURN ON INVESTMENT

You can measure the Return on Investment (ROI) for a PPC campaign. If you exceed your budget, a PPC campaign can be cancelled at any time. To determine your starting budget, you need to decide how much a PPC conversion (a visitor becomes a customer) is worth in profit to your business, how many additional sales leads your company is ready to handle, your conversion rate (provided by your PPC company), and what your conversion goal is. The formulas below will help establish your budget:

- Number of Conversions = Sales leads per day x Percent of conversion x 20 work days in month

- PPC Budget Maximum = $ in Profits per conversion x Number of conversions

- PPC Profit = Total Profit from PPC campaign – Total Budget for PPC

Let us assume you make an average of $100 net profit per conversion, you can process 100 sales leads per day, and your conversion rate is 20 percent (20 percent of all click-throughs culminate in a sale). Based on an average 20-workday-month, this gives you a net profit of $4,000 per month that can be spent on your PPC campaign.

Number of conversions = 100 x 20% x 20 = 400

PPC Budget Maximum = $100 x 400 = $4,000

If you then pay out $2,000 for your PPC advertising campaign for one month of PPC service and receive 500 leads that convert into 100 conversions (20 percent conversion rate), you are realizing $8,000 profit on your advertising campaign costs, resulting in an overall 400 percent ROI.

PPC Profit = $10,000 – $2,000 = $8,000

Keep in mind your actual sales figures will change monthly, based on actual conversions.

NEGATIVE CAMPAIGN KEYWORDS

Negative keywords prevent your ads from appearing for queries containing the keywords you have specified. This is particularly useful when you are trying to limit the number of times your ad may appear based on specific keywords. Since Google AdWords supports negative campaign keywords, this feature is available in your Google AdWords account.

8

INCREASE PROFITS WITH GOOGLE ADSENSE

I have given you a comprehensive introduction to Google AdWords, and now we will take a look at other marketing tools offered by Google. Google AdSense lets you place Google advertisements on your Web pages, earning money for each click by site visitors. Instead of paying per click, you actually earn revenue per click, just for hosting the ads on your Web site. There are dozens of books published about Google AdSense, and most claim if you implement Google AdSense correctly you can just sit back and watch the profits roll in. This may or may not be the case, and recently Google has changed the terms and conditions of AdSense, placing stricter limitations on the revenue potential. That said, it is a proven alternative income stream that can be used in conjunction with, or independent of, pay-per-click or other Google marketing techniques.

Google.com states that "Google AdSense is the program that can give you advertising revenue from each page on your Web site — with a minimal investment in time and no additional resources. AdSense delivers relevant text and image ads that are precisely targeted to your site and your site content. And when you add a Google search box to your site, AdSense delivers relevant text ads that are targeted to the Google search results pages generated by your visitors' search request."

The concept of Google AdSense is very simple: You earn revenue potential by displaying Google ads on your Web site. Essentially, you become the host site for someone else's pay-per-click advertising. Since Google puts relevant CPC (cost-per-click) and CPM (cost-per-thousand impressions) ads through the same auction and lets them compete against one another, the auction for the advertisement takes place instantaneously, and Google AdSense subsequently displays a text or image ad(s) that will generate the maximum revenue for you.

Becoming an AdSense publisher is very simple. You must fill out a brief application form online at **https://www.google.com/AdSense/**, which requires your Web site to be reviewed before your application is approved. Once approved, Google will e-mail you HTML code for you to place on your Web pages. When the HTML code is saved onto your Web page, it activates and targeted ads will be displayed on your site.

You must choose an advertisement category to ensure only relevant, targeted advertisements are portrayed on your Web site. Google has ads for all categories of businesses and for practically all types of content, no matter how broad or specialized.

The AdSense program represents advertisers ranging from large global brands to small and local companies. Ads are also targeted by geography, so global businesses can display local advertising with no additional effort. Google AdSense also supports multiple languages.

You can also earn revenue for your business by placing a Google search box on your Web site — literally paying you for search results. This service may help keep traffic on your site longer since visitors can search directly from your site. The feature is also available to you at no cost and is very simple to implement.

Google states that their "ad review process ensures that the ads you serve are not only family-friendly, but also comply with our strict editorial guidelines. We combine sensitive language filters, your input, and a team of linguists with good hard common sense to automatically filter out ads that may be inappropriate for your content."

Additionally you can customize the appearance of your ads, choosing from a wide range of colors and templates. This is also the case with Google's search results page. To track your revenue, Google provides you with an arsenal of tools to track your advertising campaign and revenue.

HOW TO SET UP YOUR GOOGLE ADSENSE CAMPAIGN

The first step is to complete the simple application form, which is on the Web at **https://www.google.com/AdSense/g-app-single-1**. It is critical that you carefully review the terms of service. In particular, you must agree that you will:

- Not click on the Google ads you are serving through AdSense

- Not place ads on sites that include incentives to click on ads

In other words, you cannot click on your ads, have others click on your ads, or place text on your Web site asking anyone to click on your ads.

Screenshots (C) Google Inc. and are reproduced with permission.

When your Web site is reviewed and your account is approved, you will receive an e-mail like the one below:

ADSENSE APPROVAL E-MAIL

Your Google AdSense application has been approved. You can now activate your account and start displaying Google ads and AdSense for search on your site in minutes.

To quickly set up your account, follow the steps below. Or, for a detailed video walkthrough, view our Getting Started tutorial:

http://www.google.com/AdSensewelcome_getstarteddemo.

STEP 1: Log in to your account.

Visit **https://www.google.com/AdSense?hl=en_US** and log in using the 'Existing Customer Login' box at the top right. If you've forgotten your password, visit **https://www.google.com/AdSense/assistlogin** for assistance.

STEP 2: Generate and implement the AdSense code.

ADSENSE APPROVAL E-MAIL

Click on the 'AdSense Setup' tab, then follow the guided steps to customize your code. When you've reached the final step, copy the code from the 'Your AdSense code' box and paste it into the HTML source of your site. If you don't have access to edit the HTML source of your pages, contact your webmaster or hosting company.

Not sure how to add the code to the HTML source of your page? Our Help with Ad Code video tutorial can guide you through the process - find the tutorial at **http://www.google.com/AdSensewelcome_implementingadcode.**

Once the code is implemented on your site, Google ads and AdSense for search will typically begin running within minutes. However, if Google has not yet crawled your site, you may not notice relevant ads for up to 48 hours.

Step 3: See the results.

After your ads start running, you can see your earnings at anytime by checking the online reports on the Reports tab in your account. For a quick overview of your earnings reports and the 5 steps to getting paid, view our Payments Guide: **https://www.google.com/AdSense/payments**.

Have any questions? The AdSense Help Center is full of useful information and resources to help you familiarize yourself with

AdSense: **https://www.google.com/support/AdSense?hl=en_US**. You can also find the latest news and tips on the AdSense blog:

http://www.AdSense.blogspot.com.

IMPORTANT NOTES:

* Want to test your ads? Please don't click on them - clicking on your own ads is against the AdSense program policies (**https://www.google.com/adsguide/policies**). Instead, try the AdSense preview tool, which allows you to check the destination of ads on your page without the risk of invalid clicks. For additional information, or to download the AdSense preview tool, please visit **https://www.google.com/support/AdSense/bin/topic.py?topic=160**.

* You can add the code to a new page or site at any time. Please keep in mind, however, that we monitor all of the web pages that contain the AdSense code. If we find that a publisher's web pages violate our policies, we'll take appropriate actions, which may include the disabling of the account. For more information, please review the Google AdSense Terms and Conditions (**www.google.com/adsguide/tnc**).

GOOGLE ADSENSE PROGRAM POLICIES

Your Google AdSense campaign must be in compliance with all the program policies, which are available here: **https://www.google.com/adsense/support/bin/topic.py?topic=8423**.

Webmaster Guidelines

In addition to the standards listed in the program policies, AdSense participants are required to adhere to the Webmaster guidelines posted at **http://www.google.com/webmasters/guidelines.html**. Some relevant items from the guidelines are included below for your reference:

- Do not load pages with irrelevant or excessive keywords.

- Do not employ cloaking or sneaky tactics.

- Do not create multiple pages, subdomains, or domains with substantially duplicate content.

- Avoid hidden text or hidden links.

- Keep the links on a given page to a reasonable number (fewer than 100).

- Do not participate in link schemes designed to increase your site's ranking or page rank. In particular, avoid links to Web spammers or "bad neighborhoods" as your Web site may be affected adversely by those links.

SETTING UP GOOGLE ADSENSE ON YOUR WEB SITE

When you first sign up, you will see "Today's Earning" text, along with any action notices, such as in the screen shot below. In addition you can navigate to your AdSense setup and My Account. To set up your initial AdSense account, click on the "My Account" tab. Be aware that, because Google will be paying you, you will be required to complete several steps before your account is activated, such as provide W-9 tax data and choose your form of payment (electronic transfer or check payment). You may review/edit all your account settings, including payment options, and review payment history data from the "My Account" tab.

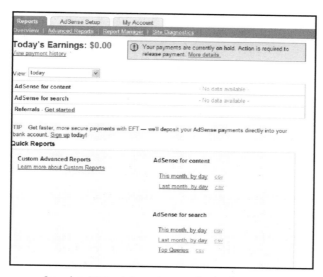

Screenshots (C) Google Inc. and are reproduced with permission.

Click on the "Account Setup" to begin setting up your advertisements. The following screen will be displayed:

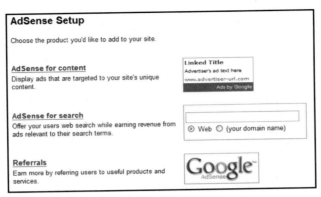

Screenshots (C) Google Inc. and are reproduced with permission.

Choose which product you would like to add to your Web site. You may choose either AdSense for Content, AdSense for Search, or Referrals. We will set up a Google AdSense for content advertisement on our Web site. You will now choose your Ad Type. You may choose Ad Unit (use the drop down menu to choose: text and image ads, text only, or image only ads). Ad Unit with Text and Images is the default (and recommended) setting, or you may choose a Link Unit, which displays a list of topics relevant to your Web page.

Screenshots (C) Google Inc. and are reproduced with permission.

You will be presented with several options to choose from, including unit format, colors, and other options. Choose your desired options using the drop down menus. This is not the actual advertisement that will be displayed on your Web site, but merely a sample of how it may appear.

Screenshots (C) Google Inc. and are reproduced with permission.

You may use "More Options" to enable Custom Channels or elect to alternate ads or colors, including the option to show public service ads if there is no advertisement ready to be displayed on your Web site. Publishers often report large increases when they change the format, color, and placement of their ads. Channels allow you to better analyze your results. With channels, you can look at different factors, such as the performance of sites, sections of sites, and ad units. AdSense records every channel impressions, click through rate, cost per thousand, and earnings statistics.

Source: **https://www.google.com/adsense/support/bin/answer.
py?hl=en&answer=32614**

After choosing your selections, you will be provided with HTML code that simply needs to be placed in the HTML code on your Web site. You are free to place the code on one or many pages within your Web site.

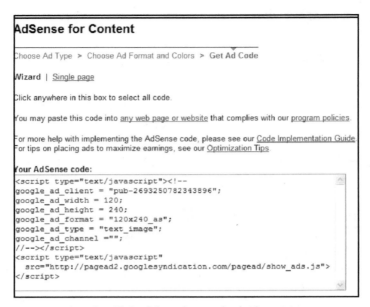

Screenshots (C) Google Inc. and are reproduced with permission.

When you insert the HTML code into your Web site, your campaign is activated and advertisements are immediately served to your site. Remember: Do not click on your advertisement at any time, even to "test" them. Google provides a preview mode for testing.

Screenshots (C) Google Inc. and are reproduced with permission.

An article you might find useful is "Five Ways to Improve Your AdSense

Earnings" by John Ugoshowa. It can be found at **http://www.articlealley. com/article_163190_81.html.**

Another article you may consider reading is "Google AdSense Profit: Three Steps to Triple Your AdSense Earnings" by Shannon Baker. It can be found at **http://www.articlealley.com/article_77899_3.html.**

HOW TO SET UP YOUR GOOGLE REFERRALS

Google AdSense program policies allow you to place one referral per product, for a total of up to four referrals, on any page. You simply click on the referral link to choose your referrals.

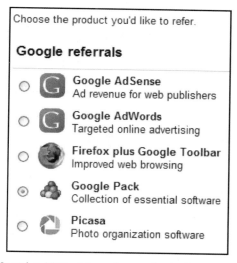

Screenshots (C) Google Inc. and are reproduced with permission.

Google AdSense will generate the HTML code for your Web site. Once the code is placed on your Web pages, your referral will be activated and displayed on your Web site as shown below. You have a variety of options in size, color, and wording, and you can change your referral advertisements at any time.

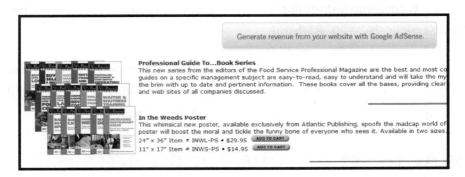

Screenshots (C) Google Inc. and are reproduced with permission.

Google AdSense is simple to implement, non-intrusive, and allows you to open channels to new potential revenue for your business.

HINTS AND TIPS FOR MAXIMIZING GOOGLE ADSENSE ON YOUR WEB SITE

Google AdSense is an outstanding way to generate Web site traffic, attract advertisers, and create a revenue stream for your business. Use these hints and tips to maximize your earning potential:

- Always follow the Google AdSense guidelines.

- Do not modify or change the Google AdSense HTML code you place on your Web site.

- Do not use colored backgrounds on the Google AdSense ads. If you have a Web site with a colored background, modify the advertisement to match your background.

- Place your ads so they are visible. If someone needs to scroll down to see your ads, you will likely not get any clicks on them. Play with the placement to maximize visibility.

- Do not include incentives for anyone to click on your ads (i.e., click here, click on my ads). This is also a violation of the Google AdSense guidelines. Do not have friends, family, or co-workers click on the advertisements.

- Do not click on your own ads. Do not reload your browser and click on your ads; do not test your ads by clicking on them.

- Do not place ads in pop-up windows.

- Do not buy an "AdSense Template Web Site," which is readily available on eBay and other online marketplaces. These "get rich click" campaigns are against Google's policies and do not make money.

- Text ads typically do better than image ads. If you insist on image ads, keep them reasonable. I recommend only using the 300x250 medium rectangle.

- You can modify the URL link color in the advertisement through the Google AdSense account panel. This makes it stand out and attracts the eye of the site visitor.

- If you have a blog, use it for advertisements as well. You need to get Google approval for your blog, and when you do, this is a successful area to insert advertisements.

- If your Web site has articles on it that you wish to embed advertisements in, use these guidelines: Short articles — place the ad above the article. Long articles — embed it in the content of the article.

- Wider format advertisements are more successful. The paying advertisement format is the large rectangle.

- Distribute ads on each Web page. Combine ads with referrals and search boxes so your Web site does not look like a giant billboard.

- Put the Google search box near the top righthand corner of your Web page.

- If your advertisements are based on content, the first lines of the Web page determine your site content for ad serving purposes.

- Set the Google AdSense search box results window so that it opens in a new window. This will keep your browser open, and they will not navigate away from your Web site.

Read more about this topic in the following two articles: "How to Make Money Using Google AdSense" by Joe Singer — **http://www.articlealley.com/article_130077_80.html** — and "Maximize Revenue from Google AdSense" by Monica Corral-Lorica — **http://www.articlealley.com/article_85378_7.html.**

CASE STUDY: HOW TO CREATE GOOGLE ADSENSE PAGES

By Paul Bliss
www.SEOforGoogle.com

First let me preface this article by stating that you should NOT create pages for the "gaming" of AdSense. Most companies who use AdWords are small to medium sized businesses trying to grow.

With rampant click fraud, those advertisers won't be able to advertise, and AdSense won't pay out as well.

That said, let's begin the process.

For our example, our topic is that of "widgets," so where do get started?

Create the page. Sounds simple enough, but there are some coding standards you should always use. They are:

CASE STUDY: HOW TO CREATE GOOGLE ADSENSE PAGES

- Name of the page — Use the name of the keyword you are targeting. So, in this example it would be widget.htm. You can use your Web server's technology as well, but if in doubt, you can never go wrong with the .htm.

- Title the page — Use the keyword again for the title.

- Meta Tags — Yes, they are still used. Make sure you include the keywords in your meta keyword list, and give a definition of the word in your meta description tag.

- H1 — Put your keyword in stylized H1 tags. Use CSS to make the tag look consistent with the rest of your site.

Content — This is often the biggest obstacle non-writers have. Don't worry; follow these steps and you'll soon be on your way to original content.

- Go to MSN, Yahoo, and Google

- Enter your keyword into the search box

- Look at the top five sites listed from each search engine

- Educate yourself on the topic from the content found on these sites

Page Copy — Now that you've absorbed more information, compose your own page of ORIGINAL content. You can take bits and pieces from the other pages, but be sure to inject your personality into your writing. That will make it uniquely yours.

Links — Don't forget to link to authority sites about your subject. It's very natural for Web pages to have links to other sites; don't forget about this key point. Take a moment to see why you need outbound links.

Traffic — The most obvious is getting traffic to your site. Your site will have higher paying ads if your page gets more traffic. If you need help with this, be sure to visit the SEO resources section.

Personally, I tried using the traffic generating sites, and quite frankly, they are a waste of time. Sure, you'll build up your traffic numbers, but it's usually from an autosurfing program.

Here's a great article on what to watch for and how click fraud is committed: **http://www.sofizar.com/google-adsense-fraud.php**.

I hope you have better luck than I did.

CASE STUDY: HOW TO CREATE GOOGLE ADSENSE PAGES

Paul Bliss has been optimizing sites for over seven years and has successfully ranked over 80 clients into top ranked positions on Google. He is a Certified eMarketer and is the author of the ebook SEO for Google, *which explains how to get your site top rankings in Google.*

9

HOW TO IDENTIFY & COMBAT PAY-PER-CLICK FRAUD

Google AdWords pay-per-click advertising can be extraordinarily profitable and, if managed correctly, will dramatically increase your customer base and potential revenue by driving targeted visitors to your site. Once you master the techniques of pay-per-click advertising, your biggest challenge will be how to recognize and combat fraud.

Whenever I discuss pay-per-click fraud with clients, they envision a competitor clicking on their advertisement every now and then just to drive up costs or someone who inexplicably clicks on your ad over and over again until they become bored and move on to some other unsuspecting advertiser. Unfortunately, I am referring to a well thought out, organized, targeted, technologically advanced, and highly destructive automated process of creating applications, scripts, and robots, which will continue to generate thousands upon thousands of clicks using ingenious techniques to disguise their identify with IP spoofing (and many others), all designed to cost you thousands of dollars in fraudulent clicks while hiding behind a false identity.

However: Realize you will not sell a product with every click on your advertisement. If you have ten clicks today on your advertisement and sell two products as a direct result of those clicks, your conversion rate is 20 percent. Remember that most PPC providers provide you with free tools to automate the tracking of your conversion rates. Some of these reasons for low conversion may include:

- Not interested in your products

- Turned off by your Web page or Web site

- Were not able to find enough information about your product on your Web site

- Price

- Brand

- Availability

- Competition

- Technical problems (i.e., your shopping cart is not working)

WHAT IS FRAUD IN RELATION TO PPC MARKETING?

Clickfraud.com reports that, by 2008, click fraud will reach an estimated $1.6 billion, a 45 percent increase over the $1.1 billion in 2005. It was also noted that:

- In 2004, at least $500 million in PPC online advertising expenditure was wasted through click fraud.

- By 2008, the estimated cost of click fraud to online advertisers will be in excess of $1.6 billion.

- As much as 70 percent of annual online advertising spending is wasted because of click fraud.

- Corrupt affiliates of ad networks such as Google and Yahoo account for 85 percent of all click fraud.

Source: **http://www.mediabuzz.com.sg/e-marketing-web-stories/click-fraud-still-a-cat-and-mouse-game.html**

PPC fraud is typically the result of:

- Unscrupulous PPC traffic and content partners of PPC search engines and directories. These companies gain financially based on the volume of referral traffic to their partner and may resort to fraudulent methods to obtain them.

- Competitors who attempt to break your budget by clicking away on your ad, quickly consuming your budget with no sales conversion.

- WebBots, spiders, and crawlers designed to generate fraudulent clicks and consume your budget maliciously with no sales conversion.

You need to understand the following facts:

- Search-engine companies, PPC providers, and advertisers agree that click fraud exists.

- Search-engine companies and PPC providers agree that PPC advertisers should not be billed for fraudulent click activity.

- Search-engine companies have stated that they have effective click fraud protection built into major search engines.

TIPS AND SUGGESTIONS TO COMBAT FRAUD

Here are some tips and suggestions for combating click fraud without breaking your budget:

- Keep current with published anti-click fraud tips and suggestions.

- Do your research when selecting a PPC provider. While there are many reputable providers, review their policies and tools for combating fraud before you sign up.

- Do not sign up with PPC companies that allow "incentive sites." An incentive site is typically one that offers free products, free competitions, or junk promotions.

- Monitor click-through rates.

- Review your Web site traffic reports.

- Place daily click limits in your campaign.

- Establish a daily budget to limit your total costs per day.

- Limit your ad to your target geographic audience. There is no need to display your Google ad in Russia if you do not do business there.

- Review your IP referral logs, usually provided by your Web site hosting company or Google. If you have multiple clicks from the same IP address, you are likely the victim of fraud.

- Report potential fraud to Google.

- Consider an advanced fraud detection tool.

A few articles I recommend for learning more about click fraud are:

- "Click Fraud: Six Things You Should Be Aware of Before You Buy 'Guaranteed Traffic,'" by John Young, available at **http://www.articlealley.com/article_89257_3.html**

- "Google's Click Fraud Woes," by Peter Elmer, available at **http://www.articlealley.com/article_83210_7.html**

- "Google and Yahoo to Settle Click Fraud Cases," by Michael Goldstein, Esq, available at **http://www.articlealley.com/article_73826_18.html**

CASE STUDY: WHITE PAPER — HOW TO DEFEND YOUR WEB SITE AGAINST CLICK FRAUD

By Dmitri Eroshenko and Michael Bloch
Reprinted with permission of Clicklab.com and Michael Bloch

Click fraud is a problem that can seriously undermine your PPC advertising efforts. This white paper expands on what we know about click fraud and outlines the steps you can take to protect your investment:

- What do you really need to know about PPC advertising

- Who's behind the different types of click fraud

- Using scoring algorithm to detect and document click fraud

- Measuring your traffic quality with Click Inflation Index (CII)

PPC Advertising in a Nutshell

Pay-per-click is a paid inclusion model used by some search engine companies that usually requires you to bid on words (keywords) or phrases (keyphrases) that your target market might use when performing searches. The highest bidder gets the top ranking in the search results, with the next highest bid below and so on. Each time a listing is clicked on, the bid amount is subtracted from the advertisers' deposit.

Some companies charge a flat rate per click, so there's no actual bidding. In this model, ranking is determined by the perceived quality of the page as calculated by

CASE STUDY: WHITE PAPER — HOW TO DEFEND YOUR WEB SITE AGAINST CLICK FRAUD

a ranking algorithm. When this model is used, it then becomes particularly important to ensure that landing pages are optimized for search engines. In fact, regardless of the PPC model, considering the investment you are making, you should ensure your site is as close to perfect as possible in every aspect in order to achieve maximum conversions.

Pay-per-click is an excellent marketing strategy as it can send very targeted clients to your site, but it can also be a budget black hole. Before you launch a PPC campaign, you'll first need to perform some calculations for projected ROI (Return on Investment).

Calculating the Cost

You should first calculate your current visitors/sales ratio. If one Web site visitor out of a hundred currently purchases your product, then bidding $0.10 per click will cost you an estimated $10 per sale. If your profit margin is $15 per sale, then it may be viable. If it's $9, then it's just not worth it. This is just a rough guide, but a good rule of thumb to work by.

Be Cautious of PPC Bidding Wars

Some PPC advertisers, through either aggressive marketing strategies, Ignorance, or "auction fever," engage in a bidding war for the no.1 spot — keep well clear of these scenarios. In very competitive markets, it's not unusual to see a difference of many dollars between the no.1 and no.2 rank bids. Given that not everyone who clicks on a listing will purchase, it can become an extraordinarily expensive marketing exercise to be no.1. Positions 2 to 5 may still perform well in terms of sending converting traffic to you.

Keyword Targeting

You may also find it more economical to bid on more targeted keywords and phrases that aren't quite as popular. For example, a search on "freebsd Web hosting" on a leading PPC search engine showed that the top bidder only pays $0.10 for each click; a difference of over $8.30 on the term "Web hosting." Using this strategy will cut down your advertising costs and the more refined targeting may generate improved conversion rates. Searchers who are clear on what they wish to buy tend to be tend to be specific in their search criteria. The novice searcher and "tire-kickers" tend to be more generalized in the search terms they use. If you bid on generic terms, you'll be paying the bill while they are learning to refine their queries. Using a tool such as Clicklab will help you in refining your keyword lists by identifying the words and phrases that actually result in conversions.

CASE STUDY: WHITE PAPER — HOW TO DEFEND YOUR WEB SITE AGAINST CLICK FRAUD

Choosing a PPC Search Engine

Hundreds of pay-per-click search engines have sprung up in recent years, but very few of them will actually deliver traffic, regardless of what their promotion states. A few companies, such as Overture and Google, account for the vast majority of PPC traffic. PPC search engines extend network coverage by offering other site owners search boxes/feeds under a revenue share (affiliate) arrangement. The site owner is paid for each search carried out via their site, or for each click a search generates. The better pay-per-click engines have networks consisting of thousands of good quality sites where your listings can appear.

Things to Look for in a PPC Company

- Tools. Does the company offer keyword suggestion features and extensive reporting?

- Coverage. Who uses their data feeds?

- Cost. Are there setup fees or minimum balances? What is the minimum bid?

- Support. Try out their e-mail support — ask a few questions before signing up. If they are slow in responding during the pre-sales process, you can practically guarantee that after sales support will be shocking.

- Click fraud. This costs advertisers millions of dollars each year..

Ask what type of anti-click fraud strategies the company has implemented. Will the company investigate fraud aggressively and compensate you where click fraud is proven? It's also wise to invest in an external monitoring system such as Clicklab. Clicklab's advanced analytics engine will flag instances of click fraud that occur in your campaigns. There's no doubt that PPC advertising can be very profitable, but click fraud is probably the most ignored yet potentially most expensive and damaging aspect of PPC that advertisers need to be very familiar with.

What Is Click Fraud?

Online advertising fraud has been around from the early days of the Internet. To justify the expensive rates and create additional inventory, shady publishers devised the means of artificial inflation of impressions and click-throughs to advertisers' Web sites. Today, click fraud refers to the premeditated practice of clicking on pay-per-click ads without the intent to buy advertisers' products or services or take other actions. Essentially, click fraud is the practice where a person or persons systematically clicks

CASE STUDY: WHITE PAPER — HOW TO DEFEND YOUR WEB SITE AGAINST CLICK FRAUD

on links, or uses software to do so, to either garner a profit for themselves through click commissions or to purposefully deplete the PPC funds of a competitor.

Who Engages in Click Fraud?

Click fraud can be as minor as an affiliate who clicks on an ad once a day to bump up his revenues, or a competitor who occasionally clicks on an ad out of spite. Major click fraud is very well organized, fleecing millions of dollars from advertisers each year. Some fraudsters create complex robots (software) to generate thousands of clicks, while spoofing IP addresses in order to avoid detection.

There are also ready-made software products, freely available on the market, for generating false clicks. For example, SwitchProxy, a third party extension for Mozilla Firefox browser, allows anyone to click on the same paid links repeatedly from a different IP address (that of a proxy server) without ever switching an Internet connection. Still too much work? There are commercial tools you can download, such as FakeZilla (fakezilla.com) and I-FAKER (ifaker. com), based in Bulgaria and Ireland.

Other fraudsters employ teams of people in developing countries to click on ads. This may sound a little extreme but with some click bids as high as $10 to $20 each, and if you only have to pay someone $5 a day to click on links, this strategy can be very profitable for the fraudster. In March of this year a 32-year-old California man was arrested and charged with extortion and wire fraud in connection with the software he developed called Google Clique. Google Clique was designed to automatically click on paid ads, while remaining virtually undetectable by the search engine.

Michael Anthony Bradley allegedly contacted Google and demanded a payoff, threatening to release it to the "top 100 spammers" otherwise. Bradley claimed that Google Clique could defraud Google of 5 million dollars in half a year's time. Bradley (or someone pretending to be him), posing under the nickname CountScubula, posted on alt.internet.search-engines newsgroup: "Google even called me to their office, I flew up, met with them, and let's just say, they are scared and don't want this software to get out, bottom line, I don't care anymore." Google wrote in its S-1 registration statement filed with the Security and Exchange Commission on April 29, 2004: "We are exposed to the risk of fraudulent clicks on our ads. We have regularly paid refunds related to fraudulent clicks and expect to do so in the future. If we are unable to stop this fraudulent activity, these refunds may increase. If we find new evidence of past fraudulent clicks we may have to issue refunds retroactively of amounts previously paid to our Google Network members."

On May 3, 2004, the India Times published a widely read article, "India's secret army of

CASE STUDY: WHITE PAPER — HOW TO DEFEND YOUR WEB SITE AGAINST CLICK FRAUD

online ad clickers." An excerpt from that article: "A growing number of housewives, college graduates, and even working professionals across metropolitan cities are rushing to click paid Internet ads to make $100 to $200 per month."

Why Do People Steal?

"People shoplift to get something for nothing," says Terrence Shulman, an attorney, therapist, corporate consultant, book author, and founder of Cleptomaniacs and Shoplifters Anonymous (CASA), a self-help support group. Shulman estimates that the addictive-compulsive shoplifters represent 85 percent of total shoplifting population of 23 million (that's one in every 11 Americans). "This group emotionally has a lot of repressed anger and often exhibits signs of other compulsive addictions, such as overeating, shopping, drug use, or gambling," says Shulman. "When caught and confronted, they will often break down and cry." The remaining 15 percent is shared between the professionals who steal for profit; impoverished stealing out of economic need; thrill seekers getting their fix; drug addicts; and kleptomaniacs, those who steal for no reason at all. Bradley "does not appear to be typical of most of the persons I have worked with," says Shulman. "His plotting and planning and brazen 'extortive' pressures on Google are different from the shy, passive-aggressive kinds of thefts I and most of my clients have engaged in."

Shulman hypothesizes that Bradley could have "rationalized that he was not hurting anybody — that Google is a rich company, not a particular person, and that they could afford it. There can also be a sense of inferiority in people who feel the need to outsmart others or 'beat the system.'"

How Widespread Is the Problem?

Instances of advertisers who have had thousands of dollars drained from their accounts in just a few hours are not isolated. Over time, even on a small scale, click fraud can add up to significant amounts of money, dramatically affecting advertisers small and large. Click fraud can also inflate cost of each click for all advertisers as some PPC companies adjust the minimum price of each click based on the popularity of the category or keyword.

Some of Clicklab clients estimate that up to 50 percent of PPC traffic in certain competitive categories is illegitimate. While that figure may be somewhat of an exaggeration as a general average, it does occur in that range in some sectors, perhaps at even higher percentages. As PPC technology has evolved, so too have the inbuilt anti-fraud mechanisms that search companies implement.

CASE STUDY: WHITE PAPER — HOW TO DEFEND YOUR WEB SITE AGAINST CLICK FRAUD

The major companies recognize click fraud as a problem that seriously threatens their businesses. The situation is somewhat similar to the battle against viruses — as a "cure" for a virus is released, a new virus appears.

Given the nature of the battlefield, it's of crucial importance that PPC advertisers have solid anti-fraud strategies in place and not to rely solely on the search company to provide protection.

Anti-Click Fraud Strategies

Fraud can be simple to minimize initially, only requiring you to choose a pay-per-click company wisely and then monitoring results on a daily basis. The increasing incidences of more organized fraudsters will require you to use special tools to monitor activity for you. The following strategies will assist you in minimizing the amount you lose to click fraud.

Avoid PPC Networks That Allow Incentive Sites

Before opening an account, always ask the company if they allow incentivized sites into their network as feed partners or affiliates. An incentives site usually offers something to its visitors in exchange for clicking on links or performing some other action. Given this model, the clicks that you'll receive from these sites will more than likely not convert as the focus of the click isn't based on interest in your product. Incentive driven sites aren't fraudulent, but it's important to gain this clarification.

Frequency Caps on Clicks

Ask the PPC company if they utilize frequency caps and what the cap is. A frequency cap is a method that will prevent duplicate clicks originating from the same IP from being deducted from your balance.

Limit Daily Spend

Start your campaign with a reasonably low daily spend limit, then increase it slowly while monitoring results regularly. As an example, let's say you set a limit of $50 a day and during the first week you average $40 worth of clicks for a 24 hour period. Then the following week, that $40 is chewed through in the first 6 hours, without an appreciable increase in sales or leads — this could be due to click fraud. By using this strategy your losses would have been minimized.

Country Filtering

What is your target market — do you really need coverage, for example, in Romania?

CASE STUDY: WHITE PAPER — HOW TO DEFEND YOUR WEB SITE AGAINST CLICK FRAUD

Also keep in mind that the majority of all types of online fraud originates in Eastern Europe, Africa, and some Asian countries.

Server Log Analysis

Study your server logs daily and check for multiple clicks originating from the same IP or range of IPs.

Display Warning Message

For dealing with the rotten apples among your competition, have your programmers write a script that will display a nice warning message after several repeated clicks to your Web site from a paid listing on a PPC search engine.

Greetings!

Thank you for your interest in our product and services.

We noticed that you visited our site more than once recently by following a paid link from one or more of the pay-per-click search engines.

Please bookmark our site for future reference so you can save a step and visit us directly.

Enjoy your visit!

IP address: 123.45.67.89

This technique can dramatically reduce your click fraud rate.

Use Specialized Click Fraud Tools

Manual fraud monitoring can be very laborious — your valuable time is probably better spent in doing what you do best — marketing, following up on leads, refining products, or developing new content. Modern third party analytical tools, unlike their predecessors, have become increasingly affordable, accurate, and easy to use. One such product is Clicklab managed click fraud detection service.

Statistical Scoring System to Combat PPC Click Fraud

Larger PPC networks have a working mechanism for detecting fraudulent clicks.

Otherwise, we suspect that they wouldn't be able to stay in business. Today's PPCs are likely to be able to weed out non-malicious bots and amateur perpetrators. But do these systems have the capacity to stop the professionals? We're not so certain. If

CASE STUDY: WHITE PAPER — HOW TO DEFEND YOUR WEB SITE AGAINST CLICK FRAUD

the history of spam-fighting is any indicator, the click inflation problem is here to stay. Define them. Score them. Own them.

In order to remain undetected, professional inflators need to closely simulate real visitor behavior and visit parameters. They know the number of page views their clicks generate is among the first things to be evaluated.

The good news is if you use statistical methods, you will be able to beat the perpetrators at their own game. Whether it's for your internal use or for negotiating a refund from a PPC provider, what's needed is a system for statistically defining and documenting fraudulent click activity. Enter the Click Inflation Index system. This system performs a variety of tests to detect fraudulent user session signatures, assigning penalty points to each offense. If the cumulative score — we call it Click Inflation Index (CII) — exceeds the threshold, the user's session is tagged as fraudulent.

This chapter explains the basic principles and tests you can use when developing your own Click Inflation Index algorithm. You will need a competent technical team armed with an adequate Web analytics solution. The process is fun and the results are well worth the effort.

Words of caution before you begin to implement a wide-scale click fraud fighting campaign: Make sure your keyword bidding strategy is up to date. Top expensive keywords remain a high-profile target for con artists. Unless your marketing strategy calls for you to engage in a bidding war — and provides the budget for it — it's a good idea to diversify and bid on the largest possible number of well-researched, lower-cost keywords.

The click-fraud detecting tests you can use include:

Test 1. Visit depth. How many page views did this particular user session generate? If it's just one, it's a good reason to lift a red flag a notch or two — but not more. Keep in mind that there could be a variety of reasons behind the single-page visits. Perhaps your ad copy isn't clear and misleads the visitors, or maybe the network connection was too slow and the user decided not to wait for the other pages to load.

Test 2. Visitors per IP. Because of the proxy servers and networks of users sharing one Internet connection, there will always be unique visitors with the same IP address. It's normal. You just need to calculate the "normal" for your Web site's unique mix of traffic sources. IP addresses whose visitor counts exceed the control group by a certain percentage are added to the blacklist and trigger a penalty.

CASE STUDY: WHITE PAPER — HOW TO DEFEND YOUR WEB SITE AGAINST CLICK FRAUD

Test 2a. Paid clicks per IP. Works the same way as Test 2, except counts only user sessions that resulted from clicking on one of your paid links. Typically, you will track these by the unique destination URLs used in pay-per-click listings, such as yourwebsite.com/?source=google.

Test 2b. No cookie — no play? Many marketers will tell you that because most bots and scripts are not capable of supporting the cookie mechanism, a user session without a cookie is a good cause for alarm. Others will say that it can't be an accurate indicator because some privacy devotees do not accept cookies and thus look indistinguishable from bots. So, penalize or not? We think you should.

Test 3. Page view frequency. Most bots travel through your site and request pages from the server much faster than humans. If a particular user session has generated a few page views in a matter of seconds, it's a good enough reason to penalize it. On the other hand, you have to be careful not to go overboard when defining your threshold. Humans can surf through your site pretty fast too.

Test 4. Anonymous proxy servers. Click thieves know that an IP address is the primary means for identifying the user session. Therefore, they need to launch their attacks from many different IP addresses. The more, the merrier. Fortunately, IP address spoofing is not a trivial task. For this reason, click inflators often channel their activity through anonymous proxy servers. Your solution is to develop and maintain an up-to-date list of anonymous proxy servers and penalize user sessions originating from them. Most legitimate visitors have no reasons to use anonymous proxies.

Test 5. Geographic origin. Now on to the politically incorrect part. You get to blacklist any country in the world you'd like. Just think of the countries from which you never have and likely never will receive a viable lead. Remember, you're not about to ban visitors from these countries to access your Web site.

You're just going about your regular business of assigning points.

Test 6 and beyond. Finesse and customize. You can devise your own triggers and assign points to them. For example, if 98 percent of your business activity occurs during normal business hours, you may want to penalize visitor sessions originated at all other times. Or you may track visits from a set of suspicious IP addresses for a period of time, and plot their activity versus time of the day. Does it follow your site's average activity patterns? It better.

Now you need to sit down with your technical, design, sales, and marketing teams. The agenda for the meeting is to: 1) decide on which tests to use, 2) come up with the scoring system for the selected tests, and 3) pick the right threshold.

CASE STUDY: WHITE PAPER — HOW TO DEFEND YOUR WEB SITE AGAINST CLICK FRAUD

To test and adjust your selections, run through the possible actions of a dozen or so hypothetical real user personas, and calculate their scores. They shouldn't trip the alarm. Now do the same exercise using personas of click-inflating robots and humans. Visits made for the sole purpose of depleting of your PPC account should trip the wire every time.

Remember, to make sure your scoring system works precisely as intended, always compare your results against a control group of unbiased traffic sources, such as Google's and other major engines' organic search results. Click fraud is a contact sport with no rules. Click Inflation Index is a defense system you can use to protect yourself and fight back.

About Clicklab Click Fraud Detection Service

Clicklab Click Fraud Detection Service is the most advanced advertiser-side click fraud detection technology on the market today. It is the result of over two years of research and development work performed by mathematicians, programmers, and SEM and PPC specialists.

Clicklab Click Fraud Detection Service monitors your Web site traffic for suspicious activity and applies a series of statistical tests to detect fraudulent click signatures. Each failed test is assigned a weighed penalty score. If a cumulative score exceeds the threshold, Clicklab declares the visitor session fraudulent and flags it for analysis and further action.

Click Inflation Index (CII) is then calculated for each PPC search engine and keyword, allowing you to adjust your bidding strategy and generate detailed actionable reports to negotiate a refund with PPC providers. Clicklab click fraud reports serve as a form of documentation from a third party service that has no vested interest in your PPC campaigns.

Clicklab was founded in 2001 as a Web analytics company that provided businesses with a smarter way to improve returns on their Web site and e-marketing investment. From their inception, they have focused on measuring and improving conversions and ROI for their clients, as opposed to counting Web site visitors. As a result, they have developed a unique blend of advanced technology and human expertise in click fraud detection and Web analytics to help online businesses succeed.

Clicklab is a privately held company with sales offices in the Washington, D.C. and San Francisco suburbs. The company's data center operations are located in Dulles, Virginia. Mr. Dmitri Eroshenko, a leading expert in Web analytics and click fraud, heads their management team.

CASE STUDY: WHITE PAPER — HOW TO DEFEND YOUR WEB SITE AGAINST CLICK FRAUD

*Dmitri Eroshenko founded Clicklab (***www.clicklab.com***) in 2001 as the first Web analytics firm to focus on marketing ROI and conversions. He continues to oversee the company's rapid growth.*

*Prior to Clicklab, Mr. Eroshenko founded several successful e-commerce related ventures. In 1996, he created Ad Juggler (***www.adjuggler.com***), one of the first online advertising management solutions. That software continues to help companies in both B2B and B2C markets manage their ads and increase profitability. In 1998, Mr. Eroshenko co-founded ISPcheck (***www.ispcheck.com***), another trail-blazing service that has allowed thousands of ISPs and Web hosting services to expand their business using PPC advertising. It was this experience that alerted him to the problem of click fraud and inspired him to develop strategies to combat it. Mr. Eroshenko co-founded Web Hosting Magazine in 2000, where he served as editor and publisher. In 2001, he launched the very successful Web Hosting Expo, a trade show and conference in Washington, D.C. Mr. Eroshenko is known as a leading e-commerce efficiency expert who has written extensively on subjects such as PPC advertising, Web metrics, click fraud, and how to improve ROI. His articles have appeared in many respected marketing publications, such a PayPerClickAnalyst, Search Engine News, and WebProNews. Mr. Eroshenko received his MS in Physics and Engineering from the Moscow Institute of Physics and Technology in 1990.*

*Michael Bloch is a marketing and development consultant with various qualifications in business, training, and assessment that complement his broad information technology, e-commerce, and Web marketing experience gained since the mid 1990s. Michael's main site, Taming the Beast.net (***http://www.tamingthebeast.net***), receives millions of visitors a year and contains a wide variety of online business tools, tutorials, and resources.*

AVAILABLE FRAUD PROTECTION OPTIONS

This list of recommended fraud protection providers will help you in your fight to combat fraud and protect your financial investment in your pay-per-click marketing campaign. Keep in mind all major pay-per-click providers have active fraud protection measures in place; however, their degree of effectiveness is difficult for you to determine. If you want to provide an additional layer of protection for your investment, you may want to consider one of these companies:

- AdWatcher (**www.adwatcher.com**) — AdWatcher is an all-in-one ad management, tracking, and fraud prevention tool focused on helping businesses automate and improve their online marketing efforts. It was developed by the team of advertising experts at MordComm, Inc. — a New York-based online marketing firm. Founded in 2003, the company has gained early success providing practical tools to help business owners get more out of search marketing. It currently also operates AdScientist — pay-per-click bid management and optimization software that helps you manage your keyword bids in all the major pay-per-click search engines.

- ClickDetective (**www.clickdetective.com**) — ClickDetective gives you the power to track return visitors to your site and alerts you immediately if there is evidence that your site may be under attack. ClickDetective uses sophisticated tracking mechanisms to determine whether visitor behavior is normal or abnormal and provides you with the tools to do something about it. The ClickDetective reports show individual clicks in real time, unlike most search engine reports, which provide only a summary of click-throughs several hours after the event. You can also set up return visitor alerts that remind the innocent repeat clicker to bookmark your site as well as alerting those visitors with less innocent intent that their movements are being monitored.

- ClickForensics (**www.clickforensics.com**) — Click Forensics 5.0 combines patent-pending click fraud detection technology with the collective intelligence of the members of the Click Fraud Network. With Click Forensics 5.0, advertisers are able to accurately measure click fraud by several attributes including search term, providers, time of day, country of origin, and conversion rates. This tool is designed to help advertisers improve the ROI of their online campaigns by using the most accurate rating methodology in the industry.

- ClickRisk (**www.clickfraud.com**) — ClickRisk is used by leading online marketers around the world to help them uncover fraudulent Web activities, to help them find the most effective way to regain their financial losses, to help them prevent future problems, and to help them optimize their marketing campaign.

- Clicklab (**www.clicklab.com**) — Clicklab provides companies with services that help them improve their returns by combining marketing and business management expertise with technology that increases sales and reduces costs. This is achieved by enhancing your campaigns and conversion rates.

10

OPTIMIZE YOUR WEB SITE FOR SEARCH ENGINES

There are several different types of search engines, including crawler-based, human-powered, and mixed. We will discuss how each one works so you can optimize your Web site in preparation for your PPC advertising campaign.

CRAWLER-BASED SEARCH ENGINES

Crawler-based search engines, such as Google, create their listings automatically. They "crawl" or "spider" the Web and index the data, which is then searchable through Google.com. Crawler-based search engines will eventually revisit your Web site, and, as your content has changed (as well as that of your competitors), your search engine ranking may change. A Web site is added to the search engine database when the search engine spider or crawler visits a Web page, reads it, and then follows links to other pages within the site. The spider returns to the site on a regular basis, typically once every month, to search for changes. Often, it may take several months for a page that has been spidered to be indexed. Until a Web site is indexed, the results of the spider are not available through the search engines. The search engine then sorts through the millions of indexed pages to find matches to a particular search and rank them based on a formula of how it believes the results to be most relevant.

HUMAN-POWERED SEARCH DIRECTORIES

Human-powered directories, like the Open Directory, depend on humans for their listings. You must submit a short description to the directory for your entire site. The search directory then looks at your site for matches from your page content to the descriptions you submitted.

HYBRID OR MIXED SEARCH ENGINES

A few years ago, search engines were either crawler-based or human-powered. Today, a mix of both types of results is common in search engine results.

Search engine optimization is a critical component to any successful Web site marketing plan. When you deploy your Web site, it needs to be optimized so potential customers can find you. While this chapter is geared toward Google-specific optimization, most of the techniques will help you achieve success in all search engines.

There are over two billion Web pages on the Internet, many directly competing with yours for potential customers — and often your competitors are selling products identical to yours. You need to take realistic and time-proven measures to ensure that your online business gets noticed and obtains the rankings in search engines that will deliver potential customers to you.

Google offers a variety of tools, techniques, and advice to help you with your Web site optimization. First, make a visit to Google's Webmaster

Central, which is located at **http://www.google.com/webmasters/**. This Web page is your portal to Google's tools and advice on how to optimize your Web site for its search engine.

Google tells you how their search engine operates and how it works in relation to your Web site. Google combines hardware and software to provide its users with speed and efficiency, which is also due in large part to the network of PCs linked together. PageRank is Google's Web page ranking system, which was developed by Larry Page and Sergey Brin. This system plays a vital role in Google's search tools.

PageRank works in the following manner: The system uses its links structure as a way to indicate a page's value. For example, a link from Page A to Page B is considered a vote for Page B by Page A. In addition, Google looks at the page that cast the vote and takes its importance into consideration. The importance of a page, however, does not matter if the content does not match the search query. Therefore, Google also uses text-matching techniques to find important and relevant pages. Google not only inspects the number of times a word appears on a page, but also takes many other factors into consideration.

Source: **http://www.google.com/technology/index.html**

GOOGLE WEBMASTER GUIDELINES

Understanding how Google works is critical to ensure your Web site is as successful as possible, and Google makes it easy for you by publishing their Google Webmaster Guidelines, which can be found at the following Web site: **http://www.google.com/support/webmasters/bin/answer.py?hl=en&answer=35769**. The following guidelines are from the site.

Webmaster Guidelines

Following these guidelines will help Google find, index, and rank your site. Even if you choose not to implement any of these suggestions, we strongly encourage you to pay very close attention to the "Quality Guidelines," which outline some of the illicit practices that may lead to a site being removed entirely from the Google index or otherwise penalized. If a site has been penalized, it may no longer show up in results on Google.com or on any of Google's partner sites.

Design, Content, and Technical Guidelines

When your site is ready:

- Have other relevant sites link to yours.

- Submit it to Google at **http://www.google.com/addurl.html**.

- Submit a Sitemap as part of our Google webmaster tools. Google Sitemaps uses your sitemap to learn about the structure of your site and to increase our coverage of your webpages.

- Make sure all the sites that should know about your pages are aware your site is online.

- Submit your site to relevant directories such as the Open Directory Project and Yahoo!, as well as to other industry-specific expert sites.

Design and Content Guidelines

- Make a site with a clear hierarchy and text links. Every page should be reachable from at least one static text link.

- Offer a site map to your users with links that point to the important parts of your site. If the site map is larger than 100 or so links, you may want to break the site map into separate pages.

- Create a useful, information-rich site, and write pages that clearly and accurately describe your content.

- Think about the words users would type to find your pages, and make sure that your site actually includes those words within it.

- Try to use text instead of images to display important names, content, or links. The Google crawler does not recognize text contained in images.

- Make sure that your TITLE and ALT tags are descriptive and accurate.

- Check for broken links and correct HTML.

If you decide to use dynamic pages (i.e., the URL contains a "?" character), be aware that not every search engine spider crawls dynamic pages as well as static pages. It helps to keep the parameters short and the number of them few. Keep the links on a given page to a reasonable number (fewer than 100).

Technical Guidelines

Use a text browser such as Lynx to examine your site, because most search engine spiders see your site much as Lynx would. If fancy features such as JavaScript, cookies, session IDs, frames, DHTML, or Flash keep you from seeing all of your site in a text browser, then search engine spiders may have trouble crawling your site.

Allow search bots to crawl your sites without session IDs or arguments that track their path through the site. These techniques are useful for tracking individual user behavior, but the access pattern of bots is entirely different. Using these techniques may result in incomplete indexing of your site, as bots may not be able to eliminate URLs that look different but actually point to the same page.

Make sure your web server supports the If-Modified-Since HTTP header. This feature allows your web server to tell Google whether your content has changed since we last crawled your site. Supporting this feature saves you bandwidth and overhead.

Make use of the robots.txt file on your web server. This file tells crawlers which directories can or cannot be crawled. Make sure it's current for your site so that you don't accidentally block the Googlebot crawler. Visit **http://www.robotstxt.org/wc/faq.html** to learn how to instruct robots when they visit your site. You can test your robots.txt file to make sure you're using it correctly with the robots.txt analysis tool available in Google webmaster tools.

If your company buys a content management system, make sure that the system can export your content so that search engine spiders can crawl your site.

Use robots.txt to prevent crawling of search results pages or other auto-generated pages that don't add much value for users coming from search engines.

Quality Guidelines

These quality guidelines cover the most common forms of deceptive or manipulative behavior, but Google may respond negatively to other misleading practices not listed here (e.g. tricking users by registering misspellings of well-known Web sites). It is not safe to assume that just because a specific deceptive technique isn't included on this page, Google approves of it. Webmasters who spend their energies upholding the spirit of the basic principles will provide a much better user experience and subsequently enjoy better ranking than those who spend their time looking for loopholes they can exploit.

If you believe that another site is abusing Google's quality guidelines, please report that site at **http://www. google.com/contact/spamreport.html.** Google prefers developing scalable and automated solutions to problems, so we attempt to minimize hand-to-hand spam fighting. The spam reports we receive are used to create scalable algorithms that recognize and block future spam attempts.

Quality Guidelines – Basic Principles

- Make pages for users, not for search engines. Do not deceive your users or present different content to search engines than you display to users, which is commonly referred to as "cloaking."

- Avoid tricks intended to improve search engine rankings. A good rule of thumb is whether you'd feel comfortable explaining what you've done to a Web site that competes with you. Another useful test is to ask, "Does this help my users? Would I do this if search engines didn't exist?"

- Do not participate in link schemes designed to increase your site's ranking or PageRank. In particular, avoid links to web spammers or "bad neighborhoods" on the web, as your own ranking may be affected adversely by those links.

- Don't use unauthorized computer programs to submit pages, check rankings, etc. Such programs consume computing resources and violate our Terms of Service. Google does not recommend the use of products such as WebPosition Gold™ that send automatic or programmatic queries to Google.

Quality Guidelines – Specific Guidelines

- Avoid hidden text or hidden links.

- Do not employ cloaking or sneaky redirects.

- Do not send automated queries to Google.

- Do not load pages with irrelevant words.

- Do not create multiple pages, subdomains, or domains with substantially duplicate content.

- Do not create pages that install viruses, trojans, or other badware.

- Avoid "doorway" pages created just for search engines, or other "cookie cutter" approaches such as affiliate programs with little or no original content.

- If your site participates in an affiliate program, make sure that your site adds value. Provide unique and relevant content that gives users a reason to visit your site first.

If a site does not meet our quality guidelines, it may be blocked from the index. If you determine that your site does not meet these guidelines, you can modify your site so that it does and request re-inclusion.

Source: **http://www.google.com/support/webmasters/bin/answer. py?answer=35769**

Detailed help is available for Webmasters on a variety of frequently asked questions and common topics at **http://www.google.com/support/ webmasters/bin/topic.py?topic=8843.**

GOOGLE WEBMASTER TOOLS

Google Webmaster Tools provide you with statistics, diagnostics, and management of Google's crawling and indexing of your site, including site map submission and reporting. These tools are critical to ensuring your site is optimized and ranked in the Google search engine. You can list your entire Web site in the Google Webmaster Tools.

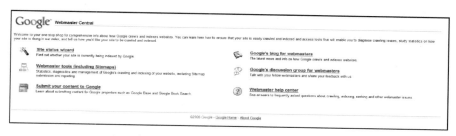

Screenshots (C) Google Inc. and are reproduced with permission.

The Google Site Status Wizard is a tool that lets you determine if your Web site is already indexed by Google. Indexing is critical if you want to be visible to customers. If your site is not indexed, potential customers will not find you in Google.

The tool is simple to use; enter your URL and click the next button. Results are displayed that notify you if the site has been indexed, on what date, and gives you potential indexing problems.

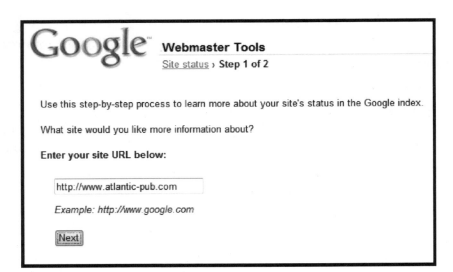

Screenshots (C) Google Inc. and are reproduced with permission.

Screenshots (C) Google Inc. and are reproduced with permission.

Screenshots (C) Google Inc. and are reproduced with permission.

Your next step is to add a "Sitemap" and "verify" your site with Google. Click on the "Add a Sitemap" link next to your Web site listing. To create a sitemap, follow the guidelines at: **http://www.google.com/support/webmasters/bin/answer.py?answer=34654&hl=en**.

Now you want to verify your site. Click on the "Verify" link to the right of your Web site listing and you will be given two options to verify that you are the site owner:

- You can upload an HTML file with a name Google specifies

- You can add a META tag to your site's index file provided by Google

I recommend you choose the meta tag option.

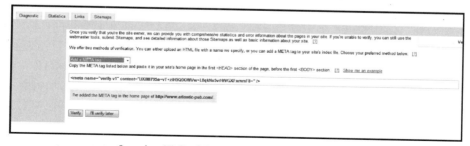

Screenshots (C) Google Inc. and are reproduced with permission.

Simply open your Web site in an editor and add the provided HTML meta tag to the head section of your Web site's home page:

```
<meta name="contactcity" content="Ocala">
<meta name="contactstate" content="FL">
<meta name="contactzipcode" content="34474">
<meta name="contactphonenumber" content="800-814-1132">
<meta name="contactfaxnumber" content="352-622-6220">
<link rel="stylesheet" href="apcnew/organized.css" type="text/css">
<meta name="verify-v1" content="UX8M795a+vT+ziH5QDOMVw+L8qkNu5vrHtVGXFxmmF8=" /> |
<style>
<!--
DIV.Section1 {
    page: Section1
}
-->
</style>
</head>
```

Screenshots (C) Google Inc. and are reproduced with permission.

After you add the Google meta tag to your home page, save your page, click the verify button, and your site will be verified.

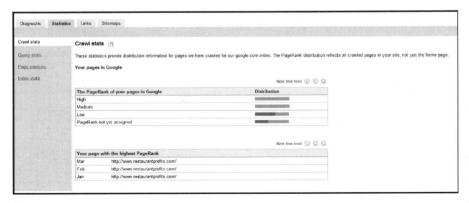

Screenshots (C) Google Inc. and are reproduced with permission.

You can now click on any of your sites to view detailed statistics. Let us take a look at one of our Web sites above. You can view detailed page ranking information, as well as other detailed analyses.

Screenshots (C) Google Inc. and are reproduced with permission.

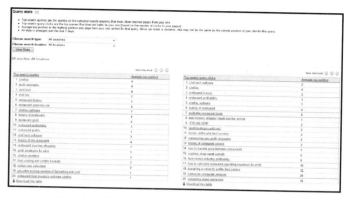

Screenshots (C) Google Inc. and are reproduced with permission.

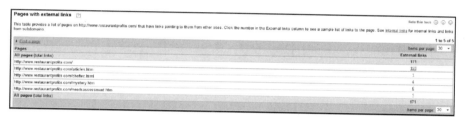

Screenshots (C) Google Inc. and are reproduced with permission.

You can use these reports and analytical results to help you better position your pages for ranking.

OTHER GOOGLE SEARCH ENGINE OPTIMIZATION RESOURCES

Google provides you with content-rich resources to assist you with SEO. You will want to bookmark and frequent the following:

- Official Google Webmaster Central Blog — **http://googleweb mastercentral.blogspot.com/**

- Google Discussion Group for Webmasters — **http:// groups.google.com/group/Google_Webmaster_Help**

- Webmaster Help Center — **http://www.google.com/support/ webmasters/**

SEARCH ENGINE OPTIMIZATION TECHNIQUES

We are now going to concentrate on some of the most popular search engine optimization techniques, which can be easily implemented on your Web sites. These include:

- Basic search engine optimization

- Proper meta tag formatting and inclusion

- Proper use of ALT tags

- Search engine registration and submission

- Search engine services

- Privacy policies

- About and feedback pages to improve search engine visibility

- Copyright pages

- Other proven Web site marketing techniques

Search engine optimization (SEO) consists of a variety of proven techniques to push up the ranking of your Web site in your target market, such as by using keywords that are relevant and appropriate to the product or services that you are selling on your Web site.

When you implement a search engine optimization plan, you use a methodology that allows you to make sure that your Web site is "visible" in search engines and is subsequently found by potential customers. Search engine optimization accomplishes this by taking the keywords that people may use to search for your products or services on the Internet using a search engine and placing these keywords in title pages, meta tags, and into the content of your Web site.

When you properly use SEO and optimize your Web site based on sound Web site design principles, you know that your Web site is ready to be submitted to search engines and that you will significantly increase the visibility and ranking within the search engines, driving potential customers to your Web site and obtaining hits you need to increase your profits and the success of your business. Focus on the content on each page and be sure to strive to include at least 200 or more content-related words on the pages of your site. Integrate your keywords into the content you place on each page, but be cautious of "keyword stuffing," which is where you overload the pages with keywords; this may result in you being blacklisted from major search engines.

Understanding the concepts and actions necessary for successful search engine optimization can sometimes be confusing and hard to grasp when you first starting using SEO techniques. There are several steps you must follow to you ensure you are getting the most out of your search engine optimization. Some of these steps include:

- Making sure that your Web site is designed correctly and set up for optimal search engine optimization

- Choosing the right keywords that are going to bring the most hits to your Web site

- Using the right title tags to identify you within search engines

- Ensuring appropriate content writing on your Web site

- Using properly formatted meta tags on your Web site

- Choosing the right search engines to which you submit your Web site and understanding the free and paid listing service options available

The main problem with search engine optimization and the number one reason most site builders fail to properly ensure a site is optimized is that it requires a significant time investment and patience. Search engine optimization will not get you immediate visibility in search engines, whereas pay-per-click advertising will. You need to be realistic in your expectations and expect it to take months to see tangible results.

META TAG DEFINITION AND IMPLEMENTATION

Meta tags are a key part of the overall search engine optimization program that you need to implement for your Web site. There is some controversy surrounding the use of meta tags and whether or not their inclusion on Web sites truly impacts your search engine rankings; however, I am convinced they can be an integral part of a sound SEO plan, and some search engines do utilize these tags in their indexing process. You need to be aware that you are competing against potentially thousands (or more) of other Web sites often promoting similar products, using similar keywords, and employing other SEO techniques to achieve a top search engine ranking. Meta tags have never guaranteed top rankings on crawler-based search engines; however, they do offer a degree of control and the ability for you, as the Web site or business owner, to influence how your Web pages are indexed in the search engines.

When it comes to using keywords and key phrases in your meta keywords tag, you want to use only those keywords and phrases that you have actually included in the content of your Web pages. It is also important that you use the plural form of keywords so that both the singular and the plural will end up in any search that people do. Other keywords that you should include in your meta keyword tags are misspellings of your keywords and phrases, because you want to make sure that search engines can still find you despite these misspellings.

Do not repeat your most important keywords and key phrases more than four to five times in a meta keyword tag. Another thing to keep in mind is that, if your product or service is specific to a certain location, you should mention this geographical location in your meta keyword tag.

Meta tags comprise formatted information that is inserted into the "head" section of each page on your Web site. To view the "head" of a Web page, you must view it in HTML mode, rather than in the browser view. In Internet Explorer you can click on the View menu and then click on Source to view the source of any Web page. If you are using a design tool, such as Microsoft Frontpage, Adobe Dreamweaver, Microsoft SharePoint Designer 2007, or Microsoft Expression Web Designer, you will need to use the HTML view to edit the source code of your Web pages. You can also use Notepad to edit your HTML source code.

BASIC LAYOUT OF A STANDARD HTML WEB PAGE

```
<!DOCTYPE HTML PUBLIC "-//W3C//DTD HTML 4.01//EN"
<HTML>
 <HEAD>
 <TITLE>This is the Title of My Web Page</TITLE>
 </HEAD>
 <BODY>
 <P>This is my Web page!
 </BODY>
 </HTML>
```

Every Web page conforms to this basic page layout, and all contain the opening <HEAD> and closing </HEAD> tags. Meta tags will be inserted between the opening and closing head tags. Other than the page title tag, which is shown above, no other information in the head section of your Web pages is viewed by site visitors. The title tag is displayed across the top of the browser window and is used to provide a description of the contents of the Web page displayed. We will discuss each meta tag that may be contained in the "head" tags in depth.

The Title Tag

Whatever text you place in the title tag (between the <TITLE> and </TITLE>) will appear in the reverse bar of an individual's browser when they view your Web page. In the example above the title of the Web page to the page visitor would read as "This is the Title of My Web Page."

The title tag is also used as the words to describe your page when someone adds it to their "Favorites" list or "Bookmarks" list. The title tag is the single most important tag in regard to search engine rankings. The title tag should be limited to 40 to 60 characters of text. All major Web crawlers will use the text of your title tag as the text they use for the title of your page in your listings as displayed in search engine results. Since the title and description tags typically appear in the search results page after completing a keyword search in the Web browser, it is critical that they be clearly and concisely written to attract the attention of site visitors. Not all search engines are alike: Some will display the title and description tags in search results but use page content alone for ranking.

The Description Tag

The description tag enables you to control the description of your individual Web pages when the search engine crawlers, which support the description tag, index and spider the Web site. The description tag should be no more than 250 characters.

Below take a look at the "head" tag from the Web site **www. crystalriverhouse.com**. The tag that says "name=description" is the description tag. The text you want to be shown as your description goes between the quotation marks after the "content=" portion of the tag; however, the full description tag may not be displayed in search results.

```
<head>
<meta http-equiv="Content-Type" content="text/html; charset=windows-1252">
<title>Beautiful Crystal River Florida Vacation Rental Home</title>
<meta name="keywords" content="Crystal River rental, Florida, Citrus County, Grouper, Fishing, vacation home, Gulf Coast rental, florida vacation, florida gulf coast">
<meta name="description" content="Casa Dos Crystal River vacation rental house & resort paradise. Located on beautiful canal off Crystal River. Crystal River, Florida is famous for its manatee watching, diving, grouper and other world class fishing trips, world class golfing and many more activities.">
<meta name="language" content="en-us">
<meta name="robots" content="ALL">
<meta name="rating" content="SAFE FOR KIDS">
<meta name="distribution" content="GLOBAL">
<meta name="copyright" content="(c) 2007 APC Group, Inc.">
<meta name="revisit-after" content="30 Days">
<meta http-equiv="reply-to" content="info@crystalriverhouse.com">
<style>
<!--
.sitecredits {  color: #FFFFFF}
-->
</style>
</head>
```

It is important to understand that search engines are not all the same and that they index, spider, and display different search results for the same Web site. For example, Google ignores the description tag and generates its own description based on the content of the Web page. Although some major engines may disregard your description tags, it is highly recommended that you include the tag on each Web page since some search engines rely on it.

The Keywords Tag

A keyword is simply defined as a word that may be used by Internet users when searching for information on the Internet and is also a critical component in developing your pay-per-click campaign. Using the best keywords to describe your Web site helps people find your site. The keywords tag allows you to provide relevant text words or word combinations for crawler-based search engines to index.

Again, although we maintain that the keyword tag is vitally important and should be included on every page, many crawler-based engines may use your page content for indexing instead of the contents of the keywords tag. In truth, the keywords tag is only supported by a few Web crawlers. Since most Web crawlers are content-based (in other words, they index your site based on the actual page contents, not your meta tags), you need to incorporate as many keywords as possible into the actual content of your Web pages.

For the engines that support the description tag, it is beneficial to repeat keywords in the description tag with keywords that appear on your actual Web pages — this increases the value of each keyword in relevance to your Web site page content. You need to use some caution with the keywords tag for the few search engines that support it since repeating a particular keyword too many times may actually hurt your rankings.

If you look at the example earlier, you will notice that the keywords tag is the one that says <meta name="keywords" content=." The keywords you want to use should go between the quotation marks after the "content=" portion of the tag. It is generally suggested that you include up to 25 words

or phrases, with each word or phrase separated by a comma.

To help you determine which keywords are the best to use on your site, visit **www.wordtracker.com**, a paid service that will walk you through the process. Wordtracker's suggestions are based on over 300 million keywords and phrases that people have used during the previous 130 days. A free alternative to determining which keywords are best is Google Rankings at **http://googlerankings.com/dbkindex.php**.

The Robots Tag

The robots tag lets you specify that a particular page in your site should or should not be indexed by a search engine. To keep search engine spiders out, add the following text between your tags: <META NAME="ROBOTS" CONTENT="NOINDEX">. You do not need to use variations of the robots tag to get your pages indexed since your pages will be spidered and indexed by default; however, some Web designers include the following robots tag on all Web pages: <meta name="robots" content="ALL">.

Other Meta Tags

There are many other meta tags that exist, but most provide amplifying information about a Web site and its owner and do not have any impact on search engine rankings. Some of these tags may be utilized by internal corporate divisions. In our example earlier you saw some examples of other meta tags that can be incorporated (note that this is not a complete list of all possible meta tags):

<meta name="language" content="en-us">
<meta name="rating" content="SAFE FOR KIDS">
<meta name="distribution" content="GLOBAL">
<meta name="contentright" content="(c) 2005 APC Group, Inc">
<meta name="author" content="Gizmo Graphics Web Design">

<meta name="revisit-after" content="30 Days">
<meta http-equiv="reply-to" content="info@crystalriverhouse.com">
<meta name="createdate" content="4/8/2005">

You may also use the "comment" tag, which is primarily used by Web designers as a place to list comments relative to the overall Web site design, primarily to assist other Web developers who may work on the site in the future. A comment tag looks like this:

<!-begin body section for Crystal River Vacation House>

ALT Tags

The ALT tag is an HTML tag that provides alternative text when non-textual elements, typically images, cannot be displayed. The ALT tag is not part of the "head" of a Web page, but proper use of the ALT tag is critically important in SEO. ALT tags are often left off Web pages, but they can be extremely useful for a variety of reasons, including:

- They provide detail or text description for an image or destination of a hyperlinked image.

- They enable and improve access for people with disabilities.

- They provide information for individuals who have graphics turned off when they surf the Internet.

- They improve navigation when a graphics-laden site is being viewed over a slow connection, enabling visitors to make navigation choices before graphics are fully rendered in the browser.

Text-based Web content is not the only thing that increases your ranking in the search engines: Images are just as important because they can also include keywords and key phrases that relate to your business. If any visitors to your Web site should happen to have the image option off when hitting your site, they will still be able to see the text that is associated with your images. ALT tags should be placed anywhere where there is an image on your Web site. It is key to remember not to use lengthy descriptions when describing your images but that you do include accurate keywords in the ALT tag. The keywords and key phrases that you use in the ALT tag should be the same keywords and phrases that you used in meta description tags, meta keyword tags, title tags, and in the Web content on your Web pages. A brief description of the image, along with one or two accurate keywords and key phrases, is all you need to optimize the images on your Web pages for search engines.

Most major Web design applications include tools to simplify the process of creating ALT tags. For example, in Microsoft Frontpage 2003, you can right click on the image, choose "properties" on the general tab, and enter ALT tag text information. To enter ALT tag information directly into a Web page, go to the HTML view and enter them after the IMG tags in the following format:

```
<img border="0" src="images/cftec.jpg" width="300" height="103" alt="Whether you're a chef, restaurant owner, caterer, multi-unit manager or other foodservice professional, ChefTec Software helps you stay on top of your business"></b></font></p>
```

OPTIMIZATION OF WEB PAGE CONTENT

Web page content is by far the single most important factor that determines your eventual Web site ranking. It is extremely important that you have relevant content on your Web pages. The content on your Web page is what visitors to your Web site are going to read when they find your site and start to read and browse your Web pages.

Not only are the visitors to your Web site reading the content on these pages, but search engine spiders and Web crawlers are reading this same content and using it to index your Web site among your competitors. The placement of text in a Web page can make a significant difference in your eventual search engine rankings. Some search engines will only analyze a limited number of text characters on each page and will not read the rest of the page, regardless of length; thus, the keywords and phrases you may have loaded may not be read at all by the search engines. Some search engines do index the entire content of Web pages; however, they typically give more value or "weight" to the content which appears closer at the top of the page.

OPTIMIZE YOUR WEB SITE

If you want to get the best results from search engines, here are some tips to optimize your Web site:

- Make sure that you have at least 200 words of content on each page. Although you may have some Web pages where it may be difficult to put even close to 200 words, you should try to come as close as you can since search engines will give better results to pages with more content.

- Make sure that the text content that you have on your Web pages contains those important keywords and key phrases that you have researched and know will get you competitive rankings and are the most common phrases potential customers might use to search for your products or services.

- No matter how much content you have after incorporating keywords and key phrases, make sure that the content is still understandable and readable. A common mistake is stacking a Web site full of so many keywords and key phrases that the page

is no longer understandable or readable to the Web site visitor
— a sure bet to lose potential customers quickly.

- The keywords and key phrases that you use in the content of
your Web site should also be included in the tags of your Web
site, such as meta tags, ALT tags, head tags, and title tags.

- Add extra pages to your Web site, even if they may not at first
seem directly relevant. The more Web pages that you have, the
more likely it is that search engines will find your pages and
link to them. Extra pages can include tips, tutorials, product
information, resource information, and any other information
pertinent to the product or service that you're selling.

- Do not use frames. Search engines have difficulty following
them, and so will your site visitors. The best advice we can give
on frames is never to use them.

- Limit the use of Macromedia Flash and other high-end design
applications, as most search engines have trouble reading and
following them, hurting you in search engine listings.

- Consider creating a site map of all pages on your Web site. While
not necessarily the most useful tool to site visitors, it does greatly
improve the search engine's capacity to properly index all your
pages.

- Many Web sites use a left-hand navigational bar, which is standard
on many sites; however, the algorithm that many spiders and Web
crawlers use will have this read before the main content of your
Web site. Make sure you use keywords within the navigation,
and if using images for your navigational buttons, ensure you use
the ALT tags loaded with appropriate keywords.

- Ensure that all Web pages have links back to the home page.

- Use copyright and "about us" pages.

- Do not try to trick the search engines with hidden or invisible text or other techniques. If you do, the search engine will likely penalize you.

- Do not list keywords in order within the content of your Web page. It is perfectly fine to incorporate keywords into the content of your Web pages, but do not simply cut and past your keywords from your meta tag into the content of your Web pages. Doing so will be viewed as spam by the search engine, and you will be penalized.

- Do not use text on your Web page as the page's background color (i.e., white text on a white background). This is a technique known as keyword "stuffing," and all search engines will detect it and penalize you.

- Do not replicate meta tags. In other words, you should only have one meta tag for each type of tag. Using multiple tags, such as more than one title tag, will cause search engines to penalize you.

- Do not submit identical pages with identical content with a different Web page file name.

- Makes sure that every Web page is reachable from at least one static text link.

- Implement the use of the robots.txt file on your Web server. This file tells crawlers which directories can or cannot be crawled. You can find out more information on the robots.txt file by visiting **http://www.robotstxt.org/wc/faq.html**.

- Have other relevant sites link to yours. We will cover the use of cross-linking your Web site with others later in this chapter; however, back linking is an often overlooked but extremely important way of increasing your search engine rankings and gaining search engine visibility.

- Consider implementing cascading style sheets into your Web site to control site layout and design. Search engines prefer CSS-based sites and typically score them higher in the search rankings.

WEB DESIGN OPTIMIZATION

Shelley Lowery, author of the acclaimed Web design course "Web Design Mastery" (**http://www.webdesignmastery.com**) and "Ebook Starter — Give Your Ebooks the Look and Feel of a REAL Book") (**http://www. ebookstarter.com**), offers valuable tips and suggestions for Web design and Web site optimization. You can visit **www.Web-Source.net** to sign up for a complimentary subscription to Etips and receive a copy of the acclaimed ebook "Killer Internet Marketing Strategies."

ESTABLISH LINKS WITH REPUTABLE WEB SITES

You should try to find quality sites that are compatible and relevant to your Web site's topic and approach the Webmaster of that site for a link exchange. Doing so will give you highly targeted traffic and will improve your score with the search engines. (Note: Do not link to your competitors.) Your goal is to identify relevant pages that will link to your site, effectively yielding quality, inbound links. You need to be wary of developing or creating a "link farm" or "spam link Web site," which offers massive quantities of link exchanges but with little or no relevant content for your site visitors or the search engines.

HOW TO ESTABLISH A RECIPROCAL LINK PROGRAM (BACKLINKS)

Begin your link exchange program by developing a title or theme that you will use as part of your link request invitations. Your title or theme should be directly relevant to your site's content. Since most sites use your provided title or theme in the link to your Web site, be sure you include relevant keywords to improve your Web site optimization and search engine rankings. Keep track of your inbound and outbound link requests. Begin your search for link exchange partners by searching a popular engine, such as Google, and entering key phrases, such as link with us, add site, suggest a site, add your link, and so on. If these sites are relevant, they are ideal to being in your reciprocal link program since they too are actively seeking link partners. Make sure that the Webmasters of other sites actually link back to your site, as it is common that reciprocal links are not completed. If they do not link back to you in a reasonable time, remove your link to them, as you are only helping them with their search engine rankings.

You may want to use **www.linkpopularity.com** as a free Web source for evaluating the total number of Web sites that link to your site.

FREE LINK POPULARITY REPORT FOR ATLANTIC PUBLISHING COMPANY (WWW.ATLANTIC-PUB.COM)	
Google	981 links
MSN	680 links
Yahoo!	661 links

USING A SEARCH ENGINE OPTIMIZATION COMPANY

If you are not up to the challenge of tackling your Web site search engine optimization needs, it may be to your benefit to hire a search engine optimization company so that the optimization techniques you use are properly implemented and monitored. There are many search engine optimization companies on the Internet that can ensure that your rankings in search engines will increase when you hire them. Be wary of anyone who can "guarantee" top ten rankings in all major search engines: These claims are baseless. If you have the budget to hire a search engine optimization company, (a) you will know that experts are taking care of you, and (b) you can focus your energies on other important marketing aspects of your business. To find a search engine optimization company, follow these basic rules:

- Look at the business reputation of the SEO companies. Ask the company for customer references that you can check out on your own. You can also contact the Better Business Bureau in their local city or state to confirm their reputation at **www.bbb.org**.

- Do a search engine check on each company to see where they fall into the rankings of major search engines such as AOL, MSN, and Google. If the company that you are thinking about hiring does not rank high in these search engines, how can you expect them to launch you and your business to the top of the ranks?

- Choose a SEO company that actually has people working for them and not just computers. While computers are great for generating the algorithms that are needed to use search engine programs, they cannot replace people when it comes to doing the market research needed to ensure that the company uses the right keywords and key phrases for your business.

- You need to make sure that the search engine optimization company uses ethical ranking procedures. There are some ranking procedures that are considered unethical, and some search engines will ban or penalize your business Web site from their engines if they find out that you, or the search engine optimization company that you have hired, are using these methods. Some of these unethical ranking procedures include doorway pages, cloaking, or hidden text.

- The company should be available to you at all times by phone or by e-mail. You want to be able to contact someone when you have a question or a problem.

Once you have decided to hire a search engine optimization company, it is important that you work with the company instead of just handing over all the responsibility to them. How much control of your Web site you should allow your search engine optimization company is an area of debate. However, since you will be controlling your PPC advertising campaign, you must have control over your SEO efforts. Use these tips to work effectively with your search engine optimization provider:

- Listen carefully to the advice of the search engine optimization account manager. This person should have the expertise to provide factual and supportable recommendations. Search engine optimization companies are expected to know what to do to increase your ranking in the search engines; if they fail to deliver, you need to choose another company.

- If you are going to be making any changes to your Web site design, ensure you let your search engine optimization account manager know because any changes you make can have an effect on the already optimized Web pages. Your rankings in search engines may start to plummet unless you work with your search engine optimization account manager to optimize any changes to your Web site design that you feel are necessary.

- Keep in mind that search engine optimization companies can only work with the data and information that you have on your Web pages. This means that if your Web site has little information, it will be difficult for any search engine optimization company to pull your business up in the search engine rankings. Search engine optimization relies on keywords and key phrases that are contained on Web pages that are filled with as much Web content as possible. This may mean adding two or three pages of Web content that contain tips, resources, or other useful information that is relevant to your product or service.

- Never change any of your meta tags once they have been optimized without the knowledge or advice of your search engine optimization account manager. Your search engine optimization company is the professional when it comes to making sure that your meta tags are optimized with the right keywords and key phrases needed to increase your search engine ranking. You won't want to change meta tags that have already proven successful.

- Be patient when it comes to seeing the results of search engine optimization. It can take anywhere from 30 to 60 days before you start to see yourself pushed up into the upper ranks of search engines.

- Keep a close eye on your ranking in search engines, even after you have reached the top ranks. Information on the Internet changes at a moment's notice, and this includes where your position is in your target market in search engines.

SEARCH ENGINE REGISTRATION

It is possible to submit your Web site for free to search engines. However, when you use paid search engine programs, you will find that the process of listing will be faster and will bring more Web traffic to your Web site more quickly. Other than PPC and other advertising programs, such as Google Adwords, it is not necessary to pay for search engine rankings if you follow the optimization and design tips contained in this book and have patience while the search engine Web-crawling and indexing process takes place. At the end of this chapter we have provided a wealth of tools and methods to submit your Web site to search engines for fee. If you do decide to hire a third-party company to register you with search engines, we have provided some basic guidance to ensure you get the most value for your investment.

Submitting to Human-Powered Search Directories

If you have a limited advertising budget, make sure that you have at least enough to cover the price of submitting to the directory at Yahoo! (called a "directory" search engine because it uses a compiled directory). It is assembled by human hands and not a computer. For a one-time yearly fee of about $300 you can ensure that search engines that are crawlers (a search engine that goes out onto the Internet looking for new Web sites by following links) will be able to find your Web site in the Yahoo! directory. It may seem like a waste of money to be in a directory-based search engine, but the opposite is true. Crawlers consistently use directory search engines to add to their search listings. If you have a large budget put aside for search engine submissions, you might want to list with both directory search engines and crawler search engines, such as Google.

When you first launch your Web site, you may want it to show up immediately in search engines and not wait the allotted time for your listing to appear. If this is the case, consider using what is called a "paid placement" program. Remember that your PPC advertising campaigns will show up with the top search engine rankings, based on your keyword bidding.

Submitting to Crawler Search Engines

Submitting to search engines that are crawlers — search engines that look throughout the Internet to seek out Web sites through links and meta tags — means that you will likely have several Web pages listed in the search engine. The more optimized your Web site is, the higher you will rank in the search engine listings.

Using Search Engine Submission Software

There are dozens of software applications that can submit your Web site automatically to major and other search engines. We have reviewed most of these products extensively and recommend Dynamic Submission (**www. dynamicsubmission.com**). Dynamic Submission, currently in version 7.0, is a search engine submission software product that claims to be a "multi-award winning, Web promotions software package, the best on the market today." Dynamic Submission search engine submission software was developed to offer Web site owners the ability to promote their Web sites to the ever-increasing number of search engines on the Internet without any hassles or complications. It helps you submit your Web site to hundreds of major search engines with just a few button clicks to drive traffic to your Web site. To use Dynamic Submission, you enter your Web site details into an application as you follow a wizard-based system, which culminates in automatic submission to hundreds of search engines

Since nearly 85 percent of Internet traffic is generated by search engines, submitting your Web site to all the major search engines and getting them viewed on the search engine list is extremely important, especially in concert with your PPC advertising campaign. It is essential to regularly submit your Web site details to these Web directories and engines. Some search engines de-list you over time, while others automatically re-spider your site. Dynamic Submission is available in four editions (including a trial edition, which we highly encourage you to try) to fit every need and budget. Here are the major features of Dynamic Submission 7.0:

- Automatic search engine submission

- Supports pay-per-click (PPC) and pay-per-inclusion (PPI) engines

- Support for manual submission

- Keyword library and keyword builder

- Link popularity check

- Meta tag generator

- Web site optimizer

- Incorporated site statistics service

Paying for Search Engine Submissions

You may choose to use a fee-based service to have your Web site listed in popular ranking directories. Also be sure to manually submit your site to the Open Directory at **www.dmoz.org**, which is free.

FREE WEB SITE SEARCH ENGINE SUBMISSION SITES

http://dmoz.org

http://tools.addme.com/servlet/s0new

http://www.submitexpress.com/submit.html

http://www.ineedhits.com/free-tools/submit-free.aspx

http://www.submitcorner.com/Tools/Submit/

http://www.college-scholarships.com/free_search_engine_submission.htm

http://www.quickregister.net/

http://www.global.gr/mtools/linkstation/se/engnew.htm

http://www.scrubtheweb.com/

http://www.submitaWeb site.com/free_submission_top_engines.htm

http://www.nexcomp.com/weblaunch/urlsubmission.html

http://www.submitshop.com/freesubmit/freesubmit.html

http://www.buildtraffic.com/submit_url.shtml

http://www.mikes-marketing-tools.com/ranking-reports/

http://selfpromotion.com/?CF=google.aws.add.piyw

http://www.addpro.com/submit30.htm

http://www.Web site-submission.com/select.htm

Note: There are many other free services available on the Internet, and we make no guarantee as to the quality of any of these free services. We do recommend you create and use a new e-mail account just for search engine submissions (i.e., **search@yourwebsite.com**).

ADDITIONAL FREE WEB SITE OPTIMIZATION TOOLS

- **www.hisoftware.com/accmonitorsitetest**
  A Web site to test your Web site against accessibility and usability: Section 508, Complete WCAG, CLF, XAG standards.

- **www.wordtracker.com**
  The Leading Keyword Research Tool. It is not free, although there is a limited free trial.

- **https://adwords.Google.co.uk/select/KeywordSandbox**
  Gives ideas for new keywords associated with your target phrase but does not indicate relevance or give details of number or frequency of searches.

- **http://inventory.overture.com/d/searchinventory/suggestion**
  Returns details of how many searches have been carried out in the Overture engine over the period of a month and allows a drill down into associated keywords containing your keyword phrase as well.

- **www.nichebot.com**
  This site has a nice keyword analysis tool, which focuses on Google's results.

- **www.digitalpoint.com/tools/suggestion**
  Gives search numbers on keywords from Wordtracker and Overture sources.

WEB SITE DESIGN AND OPTIMIZATION TOOLS

- **www.Webmarketingtoolscentral.com**
  A large variety of tools, guides, and other services for Web design and optimization.

- **www.htmlbasix.com/META.shtml**
  Free site that automatically creates properly formatted HTML META tags for insertion into your Web pages.

- **www.coffeecup.com**
  Makes easy-to-use software to design sites.

CASE STUDY: HOW TO CREATE A GOOGLE SITE MAP

Officially announced on June 6, 2005 at Google'e Blog, Google Site Map allows you to submit a listing of all your URLs for Google to crawl.

There have been many questions concerning the procedure of creating a Google Site Map. Below is the non-Python way of creating one. (Note: Google has further documentation at their site)

CASE STUDY: HOW TO CREATE A GOOGLE SITE MAP

First, create a file named sitemap.xml.

Use the following code in any HTML editor:

```
<?xml version="1.0" encoding="UTF-8"?>
<urlset xmlns="http://www.google.com/schemas/sitemap/0.84">
  <url>

    <loc>http://www.seoforgoogle.com/</loc>
<lastmod>2005-06-30T14:12:14+00:00</lastmod>
    <changefreq>daily</changefreq>
    <priority>1.0</priority>
  </url>
  <url>
    <loc>http://www.seoforgoogle.com/glossary.cfm</loc>
    <lastmod>2005-06-30T14:12:14+00:00</lastmod>
  <changefreq>weekly</changefreq>
  <priority>1.0</priority>
  </url>
</urlset>
```

Here's a breakdown of those properties:

lastmod

This is the date the document was last modified and uses the following formats:
dd.mm.yyyy
dd.mm.yyyy hh:mm
dd/mm/yyyy
dd/mm/yyyy hh:mm

changefreq -

Tells Google Sitemaps the frequency that content of a particular URL will change. Your options are "always," "hourly," "daily," "weekly," "monthly," "yearly," or "never."

The value "always" should be used to describe documents that change each time they are accessed. The value "never" should be used to describe archived URLs.

priority -

The priority of a particular URL relative to other pages on your site.

You may select between 0.0 and 1.0, where 0.0 identifies the lowest priority page(s) on your Web site and 1.0 identifies the highest priority page(s) on your Web site.

CASE STUDY: HOW TO CREATE A GOOGLE SITE MAP

Add as many pages as there are in your Web site.

Google Sitemap supports up to 50,000 pages per XML file.

Once you've completed all of those steps, you'll need to submit your site map page.

Submit to: (requires gmail account) **https://www.google.com/webmasters/sitemaps/login**

Paul Bliss
www.SEOforGoogle.com

Paul Bliss has been optimizing sites for over seven years and has successfully ranked over 80 clients into top ranked positions on Google. He is a Certified eMarketer and is the author of the ebook SEO for Google, *which explains how to get your site top rankings in Google.*

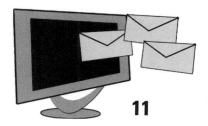

11

GOOGLE BASE & FROOGLE

In this chapter we will take a look at Google Base and Froogle. Google Base and Froogle are similar in concept; in fact, Base has replaced Froogle, although both still exist. I recommend you submit your products directly to Google Base, since they will also be displayed in Froogle. Base will eventually replace Froogle, and the front-end interface for Base has replaced the interface for Froogle. The key concept for Google Base is that it is the interface where you add your products, and you can search for products in Google Base; however, the intent is that the Base database will be incorporated into other Google tool results, such as the Google Search Engine and Google Maps. This is important because it means you can potentially load all your products into Google Base and have them available (for free) on the Google search engine and in other Google applications.

GOOGLE BASE

Google Base is an online database offered by Google that allows you to add your products in a preset format and feature your products on the Google search engine. Google Base is free, and you can submit up to 15 files to the site in these formats: PDF (.pdf), Microsoft Excel (.xls), Text (.txt),

HTML (.html), Rich Text Format (.rtf), Word Perfect (.wpd), ASCII, Unicode, and XML.

Google Base is a source for many products, including personals, jobs, cars, services, hotels, events, reviews, rooms for rent, and even real estate sales. There are so many products available on Google Base that it is impossible to list them all here.

Source: **www.google.com**

Screenshots (C) Google Inc. and are reproduced with permission.

By clicking on the "products" link you can narrow your search to "product" listing only, in which you are presented with a variety of sort options, including price, relevance, stores, brand, and links to view via Google Maps.

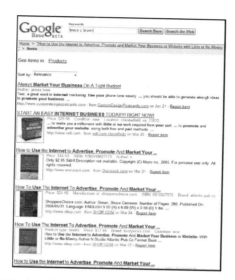

Screenshots (C) Google Inc. and are reproduced with permission.

FROOGLE

Froogle (**www.froogle.com**) is a price comparison service by Google that provides you with a Web-based form to search for products based on keywords. The results are returned with vendor information, images, prices, and so on. Essentially, you can comparison shop. As with Google Base, there is no charge to add your products to Froogle, and there is no pay-per-listing service that allows you to obtain higher results rankings. You simply submit a data file in a specified format with your product information and your products are included in Froogle search results.

Searches can be sorted by relevance ("best match") or by price (either ascending or descending). You can also search for items in specific online stores (assuming they have provided Froogle a data feed). Froogle is only available in selected countries.

Source: **www.google.com**

Froogle allows you to enter search terms, which then retrieve matching results. You can sort your results by price, product rating, seller rating, and relevance. You can compare pricing between vendors and click on the link to be taken to that seller's Web site to purchase the product or view additional information about it. As you can see below, you can also search for product by a particular seller or manufacturer.

Screenshots (C) Google Inc. and are reproduced with permission.

HOW TO USE GOOGLE BASE

To add products to Google Base, you must have a free Google account, which gives you access to all Google services in your account management page. Visit **https://www.google.com/accounts/NewAccount** to establish your Google account.

Detailed instructions for how to create your bulk upload file (Note: You can add products manually one at a time) are located at **http://base.google.com/base/products.html**. Google even provides you with sample bulk load files to help you ensure your file is properly formatted.

Below is a sample Google Base bulk upload file that is properly formatted:

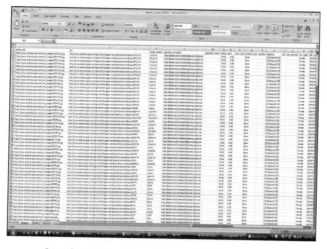

Screenshots (C) Google Inc. and are reproduced with permission.

Simply go to the "bulk upload" page to load your file into the Google Base database. Google will process and validate your file to ensure it passes all edits and controls. After your file has been processed and approved, it will tell you the date and time it was uploaded, as well as the number of active items and when the listing will expire (they are good for 30 days). Then you must upload a new bulk file.

Google will perform edits and validations on your bulk upload file and notify you via your Base control panel if there are problems with your upload. You will also be notified via e-mail. Initially your upload will show as "pending approval," and then it will change to "Approved" or "Disapproved." When your items are approved, they are visible in Google Base and Google searches. There is no commission, fees, or other charges associated with Google Base —and it is very simple to use. When your bulk upload file is created (which can easily be done in Microsoft Excel), it is essentially free promotion of your company, products, and services.

Detailed instructions on how to create and upload your Google Base items are contained in the comprehensive Google Base Help Center located at **http://base.google.com/support/**. Additional resources about Google Base can be found on the official blog **http://googlebase.blogspot.com/**.

CASE STUDY: GOOGLE BASE OPTIMIZATION

Google Base happens to be the only shopping search engine which allows merchants to define their own attributes (optional fields).

It is also formerly known as Froogle, and if you have any product that can be sold online, you have no excuse to not use this service. It's free, and Google is trying to promote its usage.

If you want better results on the shopping engines, try optimizing your feed —it's no longer good enough to just post all your products and expect your listings to be found.

There is a new opportunity that can be had for online retailers, and it's known as the "Onebox" result. To learn more about this great way to drive targeted traffic, visit OneBoxer (**www.oneboxer.com**), a fantastic blog that covers all angles better than I can.

Recently, Google made more requirements on a generic level, but there may be more if you are within a specific product category:

• brand	• condition	• product type
• description	• expiration date	• title
• id	• link	
• image link	• price	

Understandably, some merchants are upset at this since they have thousands of products that now need more information, and some products may not have all of the required fields (expiration date, for example).

So how can you take advantage of this?

Some people will search by color, some by material, and others by style. All of these are fantastic opportunities to get your product in front of a consumer who is ready to buy. It will take some time to create and get all the tweaks worked out, but it is well worth it.

CASE STUDY: GOOGLE BASE OPTIMIZATION

Paul Bliss

www.SEOforGoogle.com

Paul Bliss has been optimizing sites for over seven years and has successfully ranked over 80 clients into top ranked positions on Google. He is a Certified eMarketer and is the author of the ebook SEO for Google, *which explains how to get your site top rankings in Google.*

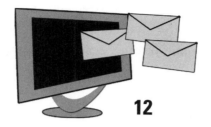

12

SUMMARY

Google is the most popular and powerful search engine in the world today. That market dominance is not likely to go away anytime soon. If Google is the most popular, it makes sense that you should put special emphasis on ensuring your site is designed, marketed, and advertised properly on Google. The goal of this book was to provide you with insight into Google, give you an understanding of the wide variety of marketing and advertising applications available, and help you achieve top rankings.

If you design your Web site properly, implement a solid SEO plan, engage in a variety of marketing techniques, and ensure that your site meets the Google Webmaster guidelines, you will see a dramatic improvement in your Web site rankings.

My goal in this book was to reveal how you can leverage Google to increase revenue, while managing limited resources, budgets, and technical expertise. This book was designed for the small business, entrepreneur, or independent Web site designer so you can save money, avoid getting ripped off, and optimize your Web site for success across all search engines.

I do recommend that you build a library of reference material to assist you with you Web site design, creation, search engine optimization, online marketing programs, pay-per-click marketing campaigns, e-mail marketing, affiliate programs, and other hints, tips, and techniques from industry experts. Reviewing the case study results of others who have succeeded and failed with Google and in other marketing ventures is a great way to learn pitfalls, mistakes, and lessons learned.

TOP EIGHT REASONS TO FOLLOW THE GUIDELINES IN THIS BOOK

- Marketing your Web site through Google is a no-brainer. It is the number one search engine in the world. You have the potential to exponentially increase your Web site traffic and sales performance.

- You can quickly reach millions of potential customers every day through Google AdWords.

- Google AdWords pay-per-click marketing is highly cost-effective. You only pay when someone is interested enough to visit your Web site.

- As your business becomes more prominent and established you gain enormous credibility in the eyes of competitors and potential customers by turning those "potential" customers into "repeat" customers.

- The Google marketing and SEO techniques I have outlined in this book are significantly less costly than a traditional marketing campaign and typically more effective.

- Google offers a wide variety of applications, Web services, and APIs — such as Google Maps and Google Earth — which are all free and can be incorporated into your Web site design.

- The Internet is becoming more and more expandable when it comes to the types and methods of advertising that can take places.

- You do not need to be a Web design master to get top rankings in Google, and you do not have to pay anyone to do it.

One last word for the small business owners, independent online retailers, or do-it-yourself Web site designers: Nothing is more gratifying than implementing the techniques outlined in this book and watching your Google ranking rise, while Web site activity increases and additional revenue is generated — as a direct result of your efforts to implement Google marketing and advertising campaigns while saving money and resources for your company. Best of luck with your Google marketing adventure. You will soon discover that Google is much more than a powerful search engine and will be an integral part of your long-term Web site design and marketing strategy.

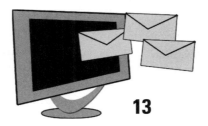

13

GOOGLE PAY-PER-CLICK MARKETING & SEO CASE STUDIES

CASE STUDY: ADVANCED MICRO-CONTROLS INC. (AMCI)

Advanced Micro Controls Inc. (AMCI) has been a leader in the design, manufacturing, and sales of industrial control solutions for twenty years. Offering a wide selection of products, ranging from rotary sensors to automation controllers, they serve the packaging, metal stamping, and factory automation industries.

With eight different product families being marketed to multiple industries, it was difficult for AMCI to know if their advertising dollars were properly distributed for the best results. Tradeshows and trade journals were becoming increasingly specialized, increasingly expensive, and measuring ROI through these channels was very difficult. AMCI's sales team was eager to find more effective methods of promoting their industrial automation controls.

In pursuit of measurable marketing, AMCI recognized the Internet's capacity as a sales tool and launched their first Web site in 1999. In the years following, **www.amci. com** produced increased sales on existing product lines and reduced tech support phone calls. At the same time, a trend analysis of AMCI's Web site results revealed that newer product lines were not enjoying the same volume of visitor traffic as their seasoned counterparts.

AMCI needed to boost their Web site's exposure on major search engines, penetrate aggressive markets, and synchronize their advertising spending with real-time marketing reports.

CASE STUDY: ADVANCED MICRO-CONTROLS INC. (AMCI)

They explored their goals and needs with IndustrialClicks.com, who helped them develop a new marketing strategy that included pay-per-click advertising. The company's sales team explained that **www.amci.com** ranked well on the major search engines for various keywords/keyword phrases; however, in the more competitive markets, their online visibility was low.

IndustrialClicks.com reviewed AMCI's Web site, becoming familiar with their products, the industries they serviced, and identified their customer base (who buys their industrial controls and how do they define value?). Once this preliminary research was done, IndustrialClicks.com began compiling keywords/keyword phrases that were associated with the company's competitive product lines. Using a search term valuator, IndustrialClicks.com identified which keywords would ultimately serve as "triggers" for the delivery of AMCI's pay-per-click advertisements.

With this collection of viable keywords in hand, IndustrialClicks.com began crafting advertising copy that was compelling and "click-friendly." Additionally, it was important that all ad copy demonstrates high degrees of relevancy, focusing closely on the target product. Generic ad copy runs the risk of driving poorly qualified prospects to the AMCI Web site, reducing the likelihood of a conversion (sales contact, request for quote, order, etc...), increasing marketing cost, and lowering the company's return on investment.

In summary, by leveraging their years of industrial internet marketing experience, IndustrialClicks.com developed pay-per-click ad copy that spoke to AMCI's industrial audience, marketing the features, benefits, and value of their products. Utilizing proprietary formatting strategies, IndustricalClicks.com enhanced AMCI's advertising click-thru-rates, while keeping their bid costs low.

Within the first three months of 2005, IndustrialClicks.com drove over 16,000 qualified prospects to various landing pages on AMCI's Web site, at an average cost of $0.10 cents per visitor. Calculating the quick math, AMCI spent $1,660.81 to promote their products to an audience of 16,176 engineers, technicians, and purchasing agents who had searched on keywords/keyword phrases closely tied to their industrial controls.

Since IndustrialClicks.com provides in-depth reporting on all of their pay-per-click advertising, it was easy for AMCI to zero in on key metrics. Data, such as their average actual cost-per-click, the number of times their ads were shown, and how many times users clicked on their ads, were accessed through user-friendly spreadsheets and e-mailed, weekly, to the sales team. This quantifiable information made it very easy for AMCI to compare pay-per-click advertising to their other marketing programs.

In review, AMCI leverages several different marketing channels: tradeshows, trade journal advertisements, and direct mailings.

CASE STUDY: ADVANCED MICRO-CONTROLS INC. (AMCI)

AMCI was leveraging multiple marketing channels, tradeshows, trade journal advertisements, and direct mailings, in support of their goals. During the 1980s and 1990s tradeshows were effective for AMCI, but dwindling attendance, escalating costs, and fewer definitive leads forced them to re-evaluate their marketing strategy. The company's tradeshow attendance was approaching an average cost of $4,000 to $6,000 and Sales was finding it increasingly difficult to justify their return on investment. While AMCI continued to participate in tradeshows nationally, they began scaling back their presence in this arena, dedicating more resources to their pay-per-click advertising online marketing efforts.

Trade journal advertising has driven industrial marketing for many years. AMCI regularly advertised in several trade publications and focused on industries such as packaging controls, electric motors, and sensors. Sales could never adequately gauge their marketing exposure, and measuring performance was very difficult. Split-testing (A vs. B testing) print ads was a slow and laborious process, requiring several months and producing questionable results at best. Additionally, promoting various products to different industries required advertising space in multiple trade publications, raising marketing costs and creating more work for AMCI.

In contrast, IndustrialClicks.com used pay-per-click marketing to promote each of AMCI's eight different product lines simultaneously, with pinpoint accuracy. The team developed over 200 segmented pay-per-click advertisements, each selling a different product with unique applications, at no additional cost to AMCI. Further, all of AMCI's pay-per-click advertisements are actively split tested (A vs. B testing) and analyzed. Data such as click-through-rate performance, ad position, and average cost-per-click drove ongoing revisions, and helped deliver a robust ROI. This type of aggressive marketing was simply not possible with printed trade journal advertising.

AMCI enjoyed reasonable success with direct mail, realizing a moderate return on investment. Unlike other forms of marketing communications, such as print ads, direct mail delivered their message straight to the buyer. At the same time, direct mail suffered the same shortcomings as trade journal ads — inflexibility, no performance reporting, and higher flat costs.

Promoting several different products simultaneously required AMCI to either sacrifice marketing focus by placing multiple products on a single advertisement or design and pay for several unique direct mail pieces — a costly and time consuming plan. From a return on investment standpoint, pay-per-click marketing is not the "all or nothing" proposition that saddles direct mail...instead, AMCI can distribute their advertising dollars across all product lines, regulating ad exposure and marketing spend on a real-time basis.

CASE STUDY: ADVANCED MICRO-CONTROLS INC. (AMCI)

Today, IndustrialClicks.com continues development on AMCI's pay-per-click advertising, empowering their sales team with expanded market reach and real-time campaign performance reporting. Moreover, IndustrialClicks.com has recently synchronized PPC campaign development with AMCI's new product releases, creating instant market awareness of the company's newest automation controllers and sensors on the Internet.

About IndustrialClicks.com
www.industrialclicks.com

IndustrialClicks.com combines pay-per-click expertise with a strong knowledge of the industrial marketplace; positioning AMCI's product marketing where today's business to business buyers shop — the Internet. Now, AMCI is reaping the benefits of Internet technology, enabling them to focus on their core strengths — engineering industrial innovations.

IndustrialClicks.com is a specialty industrial marketing company that works exclusively in the Industrial/Business-to-Business/Manufacturing sector. We develop pay-per-click (PPC) Internet advertising services that bring immediate, quantifiable results for our clients. Our expertise, in combination with this powerful sales tool, helps deliver your marketing message with pinpoint accuracy to targeted individuals. Your success will be measured by the collective number of 'clicks' your campaigns receive and, more importantly, the increase in your B2B sales orders and inquiries.

IndustrialClicks.com specializes in PPC advertising. Our goal is to deliver exceptional return on investment to industrial clients by increasing their requests for quotes and product sales. By specializing in PPC advertising, we are able to apply our in-depth knowledge of the industry, and optimize use of this dynamic marketing channel, with every client.

Basic marketing principles are the foundation of IndustricalClicks.com advertising services. Our marketing strategy is driven by research and knowledge of the target audience. We bring over five years of industrial marketing experience to our clients, promoting products and services to a variety of industries including packaging, press, and factory Automation.

IndustrialClicks.com will work with you and your technical development group to determine the most effective keywords for your product line(s). We then handle the bidding process, continually manage your keyword(s) for effectiveness, identify and re-bid new keywords/changes, monitor your competition, and run and distribute reports. Following development and implementation, the growth and quality of your pay-per-click traffic is our highest priority.

CASE STUDY: SONY STYLE

Wpromote was hired to leverage the powerful brand name of Sony and official nature of the Sony online store through optimized ads.

Wpromote created a search engine campaign encompassing the entire Sony online catalog. The goal was to match search engine users seeking specific Sony products with ads tailored to those products and deliver the user to individual product pages on the online store too.

Additionally, WPromote wanted the search engine campaign to effectively leverage the Sony brand, creating a coherent link from offline advertising to online sales. The combination of these tactics resulted in vastly improved conversion ratios, lowering cost per click by 60%, doubling the click-thru ratio, and increasing average revenue per click by 200%.

"As an established e-commerce player, we looked to Wpromote to expand the online reach of the Sony Style store and actively drive customers to the site. They launched a comprehensive campaign producing immediate results, and through constant tracking and analysis, have optimized and expanded the campaign. The results have exceeded our expectations, and the campaign built by Wpromote has averaged month-over-month sales growth of over 30%. Wpromote's support and accessibility is second-to-none. They have grown to be one of our top partners and we look forward to a long and rewarding relationship."

— Danielle Hayman, Associate Manager, Direct Marketing, Sony Electronics Inc. e-Solutions Company LLC

About Wpromote

www.wpromote.com

Wpromote has been a leader in the field of search engine marketing since its inception in 1999, working with thousands of clients from over 60 countries. One of the original firms specializing in search engine submission, Wpromote established its place online based on its superior, proprietary software, unmatched customer support, and honest approach. We have helped our clients gain visibility, gather leads, and ultimately build successful businesses with more powerful online presences. From the beginning our goal has been to seek out creative, efficient, and effective strategies to help our clients achieve their objectives online.

Founded in 1999, Wpromote is one of the world's leading search engine marketing firms. Wpromote has helped over 10,000 clients in over 50 countries achieve their

CASE STUDY: SONY STYLE

online marketing goals using proprietary, cutting edge technology, and superior personalized service. Wpromote provides expert pay-per-click management, search engine submission, and pay-for-performance marketing services.

Michael Mothner, CEO

Wpromote, Inc.
Toll-Free 1-866-WPROMOTE
Direct: 1-310-421-4844
www.wpromote.com
sales@wpromote.com
1650 Pacific Coast Highway, Suite 310
Redondo Beach, CA 90277

CASE STUDY: 1-800-FLORALS.COM

The flowers, greetings, and specialty gifts category is ranked among the top 15 online retail categories based on an average order size of $51.61. And two out of the top 10 online retailers, based on high sales conversion rates, were FTD.com and proflowers.com. What do these numbers mean to those in the floral industry? For one, statistics like these mean that more advertisers in the floral industry, like 1-800-Florals, are turning to PPC to keep an edge on the competition.

Methods of Advertising

"Our other advertising methods have included print, outdoor, radio, direct mail, e-mail, affiliate program, etc. But PPC advertising gives us greater control over driving qualified search traffic to our site based on highly targeted keywords. We control the search terms, listings, and cost in real time, adjusting for performance, seasonality, and budgeting needs," said Baxter W. Phillip of 1-800-Florals.

Starting a Campaign

Searchfeed.com allows for simple campaign setup. Phillip was able to set up a campaign for the 1-800-Florals Web site by filling out a three-step online form, and then submit keywords and listings related to his business.

"We've worked with a lot of PPC sites and think Searchfeed.com is among the most user-friendly. Setting up an account, entering keywords, and launching a campaign are a snap," he said.

CASE STUDY: 1-800-FLORALS.COM

Online Tools and Reports

"We use Searchfeed's reporting tools religiously, to monitor results, improve bid management, and drive more sales. We also like Searchfeed's Keyword File Uploader, but the most important thing is that all the advertiser tools are easy to use and easy to understand," said Phillip.

Sales Conversions

PPC advertising allows florists to change their advertising campaign based on the season or holiday, making a difference for online sales conversions.

"The cost per conversion with Searchfeed.com is as good or better than any other pay-per-click search engine out there today," said Phillip.

Cost of Running a Campaign

With a minimum deposit of $25 and minimum bid of one cent, it is no surprise that advertisers find that running a campaign with Searchfeed.com is very cost-effective.

"Searchfeed.com seems to have done a better job than others in maintaining qualified traffic over the years, and it also remains one of the more economical online advertising opportunities today," said Phillip.

Overall Results

By advertising with Searchfeed.com, 1-800-Florals was able to have their ads on sites related to their industry, resulting in targeted sales leads. For example, ads for the floral business are displayed on wedding-centric Web sites, such as **AllAboutWeddings. com**, because this is good place for consumers to type in a search related products, like for wedding flowers or wedding bouquet. This resulted in high sales conversions for a minimum campaign cost.

About SearchFeed

www.searchfeed.com

A leader in pay-per-click search engine advertising, Searchfeed.com has helped thousands of online advertisers with a cost-effective, easily tracked method of generating sales leads. Through the distribution of sponsored search results to thousands of industry specific Web sites, regional Internet service providers and emerging Web sites, advertisers receive millions of targeted leads each month while Web publishers earn revenue by delivering qualified leads.

CASE STUDY: UNITEDDIAMONDS.COM

United Diamonds distributes bridal and custom jewelry over the Internet. To attract targeted sales leads they have used many forms of advertising, and turned to pay-per-click (PPC), specifically Searchfeed.com, to boost their advertising efforts.

Methods of Advertising

"In the past, we have advertised on some comparison shopping networks and have done some minimal banner advertising that ended with poor results. In the end, PPC has been the best for us," said Bruce Larsen of UnitedDiamonds.com about why he turned to PPC advertising.

Business Solutions

Two of the main business solutions that many advertisers have derived from their online advertising efforts are an increase in targeted traffic to their site, and, as a result high conversion rates. United Diamonds.com comments below on their campaign results.

Traffic Quality

"We have a highly sophisticated Web analytics software tied into our Web server that analyzes traffic from various advertising sources. The numbers speak for themselves. Searchfeed.com has delivered phenomenal high quality traffic compared to some of the alleged big PPC advertising companies," says Larsen.

"Searchfeed.com's Keyword File Uploader has been the most useful tool for us. It allows us to create thousands of targeted keyword ads with ease. The reporting tools provided by Searchfeed.com show us, at a glance, which keywords are receiving the most clicks, and how much this is costing us," he said.

Sales Conversions

Searchfeed.com works with many niche sites to provide advertisers with quality traffic that converts into targeted sales leads for their specific industry. For example, UnitedDiamonds.com receives traffic from sites related to the bridal jewelry industry.

"Searchfeed.com traffic can be broken down into three categories: Conversions, Conversions, and Conversions. In our experience, we have some of the best conversions from Searchfeed.com visitors," he said.

Overall Results

Larsen sums up the results of his campaign simply, "50 percent of our advertising budget is committed to PPC for one simple reason — it works!"

CASE STUDY: UNITEDDIAMONDS.COM

About SearchFeed

www.searchfeed.com

A leader in pay-per-click search engine advertising, Searchfeed.com has helped thousands of online advertisers with a cost-effective, easily tracked method of generating sales leads. Through the distribution of sponsored search results to thousands of industry specific Web sites, regional Internet service providers and emerging Web sites, advertisers receive millions of targeted leads each month while Web publishers earn revenue by delivering qualified leads.

CASE STUDY: TARGETEDVISITORS.INFO

TargetedVisitors.info is an Internet advertising service. The company's marketing professional, Daniel Grossman, discusses past advertising techniques in comparison with his current search engine marketing strategies and his pay-per-click (PPC) campaign with Searchfeed.com.

"I used to spend a lot of time on traditional Internet marketing. Most of my advertising budget went to banner ads, forum sponsorships, contest sponsorships, and newsletter advertisements. These still play an important part in my month-to-month advertising, but PPC advertising has become the dominant method, and for good reason," says Grossman.

Many advertisers find that search engine marketing, using PCC technology, is a cost-effective way to generate targeted sales leads. By providing a unique form of online advertising, Searchfeed.com offers any size business a way to reach their target audience via the Web.

"Search advertising is incredibly effective. Because the Web surfer is in a search mindset and is actively seeking out my type of service, I can target these people specifically and show them that what I am offering is what they're looking for. PPC advertising has benefits other mediums can't provide. It enables me to precisely control my message, my reach and my cost on a day-to-day basis," he stated.

Online Tools and Reports — Searchfeed.com offers advertisers a wide variety of self-management tools and real-time reports that help to monitor the success of each campaign from every angle. Many advertisers find Searchfeed.com's suite of online tools helpful, especially the Campaign Cost Estimate tool, which helps advertisers assess campaign costs based on up to 5,000 campaign keywords.

"I can fine tune campaigns, or test new copy without an expensive commitment, and readily measure and compare the ROI from each campaign. If an ad isn't drawing clicks, or isn't converting, I can stop and figure out why," stated Grossman.

CASE STUDY: TARGETEDVISITORS.INFO

An important feature that keeps advertisers informed is the use of Searchfeed.com's real-time reports, which enable advertisers to immediately check how their account is performing and offers virtually instantaneous feedback about account information.

"Overall, the reports are quickly generated, comprehensive, and quickly show me where I'm spending my money and what searches are sending me the most visitors. Detailed payment history reports make recording expenses easy," he summarized.

Advertisers have access to many useful campaign tools through their advertiser interface login screen. Through Searchfeed.com's auto bid management tool multiple keyword bids can be changed simultaneously to help ensure the best ranking. Searchfeed.com's position maintenance tool ensures top position for campaign listings and helps to eliminate bid gaps.

"Searchfeed.com's advertiser interface is very straightforward and easy to use. Editing listings, changing bids, and generating reports are all a single click from sign-in, and the individual pages are intuitively easy to understand and use. Searchfeed.com's mass 'change bids' tool has been very useful and is a great time-saver, allowing me to raise listings to #1, #2, or #3 in search results without spending more per click than I'm ready to. This makes my Searchfeed.com results very easy to maintain," Grossman said.

Solutions

Searchfeed.com provided TargetedVisitors.info with an additional form of advertising that works with their current campaign by presenting an affordable way to advertise online.

"The great thing about PPC advertising compared to banner, e-mail, and other advertising methods is that you pay for performance. With other forms of advertising, I have to commit to long campaigns that may not bring a good return. Searchfeed.com allows me to control my day-to-day spending, and since conversion rates can be pretty accurately predicted after some time on a Searchfeed.com campaign, I know how many sales to expect for each dollar I spend. Compared to banner ad campaigns, the cost to acquire new customers through Searchfeed.com is lower and more predictable. Compared to other pay-per-click search engines, Searchfeed.com has a lower average cost per click while still having enough reach to deliver lots of high-quality traffic to my site," states Grossman.

Solutions — To start a PPC campaign with Searchfeed.com, advertisers simply fill out an online form with one listing, including a title, description, and keywords. Each advertiser can bid on search terms that are relevant to their site content. An account

CASE STUDY: TARGETEDVISITORS.INFO

can be up and running in no time, as most search terms are reviewed with in 24 to 48 hours and a confirmation regarding submitted search terms is provided.

In January of 2004, TargetedVisitors.info started an advertiser account with Searchfeed. com. Grossman commented about the ease of beginning a campaign, "Searchfeed. com's advertiser area is very easy to use. Becoming an advertiser was a quick and easy process. I entered my search listing, chose keywords, and funded my account with a credit card. I don't have to worry about my advertising ending prematurely thanks to automatic deposits whenever my account starts to run low."

Increased ROI — When evaluating the cost of running an online campaign with Searchfeed.com, he stated, "All of the details I need for determining ROI of my ads are a click away from sign-in through Searchfeed.com's reports area."

Customer Relations — Searchfeed.com is dedicated to developing strong customer relations and is committed to satisfying advertiser needs through the highest levels of customer service. An advertiser relations specialist addresses all advertiser needs with a personal touch.

When asked about customer service, Grossman answered, "Searchfeed.com's support team has been quick to answer my questions and to offer suggestions for improving my campaign."

Overall Results — Searchfeed.com offers advertisers the ability to reach their target audience through a simple, cost-effective method of online advertising. By providing quality traffic from thousands of leading Internet portals and industry-specific Web sites, advertisers experience high conversions and a greater return on investment (ROI).

"My conversion rate with Searchfeed.com is often greater than 10 percent. It is the single most effective advertising I've ever done," said Grossman.

About SearchFeed

www.searchfeed.com

A leader in pay-per-click search engine advertising, Searchfeed.com has helped thousands of online advertisers with a cost-effective, easily tracked method of generating sales leads. Through the distribution of sponsored search results to thousands of industry specific Web sites, regional Internet service providers, and emerging Web sites, advertisers receive millions of targeted leads each month while web publishers earn revenue by delivering qualified leads.

CASE STUDY: WOTIF SHARES SUCCESS

Matthew Varley says search marketing has been an essential element in Wotif.com's growth.

"From the very beginning, Wotif.com's board and management recognised that search marketing was an essential cost for our business. It has been the major consistent marketing cost for which Wotif.com has budgeted," Varley says, adding that "a large portion" of marketing spend is concentrated on search alone.

Varley values a search's ability to not only acquire new customers but also its ability to directly track the return on investment for each dollar spent.

"It allows us to acquire customers at a lower cost than most of the traditional marketing mediums and, importantly for Wotif.com, it operates in the same medium as our business, i.e., potential customers are already online, actively searching for our product and search marketing ensures that they find it with us instead of our competitors," Varley says.

Wotif.com worked with The Found Agency to review its natural SEO strategy as well as providing input on maximizing its rankings within the search engines.

"Natural SEO is a major part of the business going forward, and in the short time since the changes earlier this year, we've seen a large and rapid increase in growth in natural SEO traffic," Varley says.

It has also been running pay-per-click campaigns since 2001 and is constantly looking at new ways to improve the effectiveness of this medium, Varley says.

And it seems to be working. According to Hitwise's weekly rankings for the week ending May 13, Wotif.com was the number one ranked site by visits in the 'travel destinations and accommodation' category with 5.4% of market share. And four of the top 10 search terms driving traffic to travel destinations and accommodation Web sites contained the search 'wotif.'

An in-house team runs Wotif.com's entire search marketing activity, as the Brisbane-based business believes keeping this knowledge within the company is "extremely important." "Our search team is intimately aware of the business objectives and is therefore able to use this knowledge to effectively create search campaigns that are aligned with these goals.

"However, in extreme cases, such as the revamping of the natural SEO strategy, we are not averse to requesting specialist external advice," Varley adds. With competition in the travel category intense, the team has to stay vigilant.

CASE STUDY: WOTIF SHARES SUCCESS

"There are over 150 sponsored advertisers bidding on Google just for the term 'Sydney hotels' in comparison to other industries such as real estate, which I have worked in previously, where there are as little as 35 companies in the running for the most vital of terms to that industry," Varley says.

"Every week there seems to be a new travel competitor bidding on keywords within the search engines, so I do anticipate the competition to increase. However, there are also people falling out of the race at the same time. Many people seem to enter into the online travel industry, but not all of them will survive on search marketing alone."

While search marketing is the main focus of the business's online marketing activity, Varley says it has a team that is dedicated to setting up "affiliate and strategic relationships both on and off line" to ensure its success continues.

With the company soon to float, its visibility both online and off looks set only to accelerate.

About The Found Agency

www.foundagency.com.au

The Found Agency is an Australian interactive firm specializing solely in search engine marketing. Although our background includes traditional marketing, advertising, and Web design, we're now 100% focused on performance-based paid search and Web optimization aimed at high visibility in search engines.

We're young, energetic, and pride ourselves on results. We already have experience advising and implementing our unique SEM strategies for several of Australia's top 100 Web sites. We have a proven track record as a market leader in results-based search advertising and optimization, and we're keen to add your business to our list of successes in online promotion.

Fundamentally, we live for this stuff. We're driven by a passion to help our clients maximize their SEM returns, and we have the skills and expertise in internet marketing to get the best results. If your business follows our recommendations and you don't gain a healthy return on our SEM initiatives, we'd rather break our relationship with you than your trust in us.

CASE STUDY: JERRYS ARTARAMA

The business story of JerrysArtarama (JA) illustrates the benefits conferred when a company works closely with a trusted firm that can prioritize SEM (search engine marketing) within a broad range of web marketing activities.

When JA first contracted with DISC in 2003, it was a medium-sized art supplies company trying to negotiate the transition from mail order catalog sales to becoming a formidable e-commerce player. They had and still have well over 30,000 products in their database.

Over the course of three and a half years, DISC has facilitated Jerry's outstanding success by providing a full palette of SEM services including SEO, PPC, and trusted feed, as well as usability critiques, traffic analysis, and research and recommendations on a wide range of online marketing techniques. DISC has also served as an advisor and troubleshooter whenever JA's has encountered unexpected online setbacks or difficulties. JA's business metrics show the company has realized superb ROI on DISC's services.

Background

When JA approached DISC, JA's online situation was bleak: Its level of organic referrals was low, which meant that a vast amount of opportunity was being lost. Meanwhile, a larger, strong competitor in its product niche was drastically outperforming JA.

Like most companies, JA was not inclined to tackle the complexity and subtleties of SEO on its own. In fact, the company had already had a dissatisfying experience working with a large SEO firm. Not only had the investment yielded inadequate results but JA found that working with the SEO firm's account team was vexing. Part of JA's motivation to work with DISC was the fact that at a small firm it would work directly with the principals, which seemed like a less risky plan of action rather than to try another large SEM company.

At the time it began working with DISC, JA also had not yet conducted a professional PPC campaign, which it was eager to try.

DISC's Solutions

DISC started the project by conducting in-depth analysis and research, producing both an SEO Technical Report and a CMS (content management system) and SEO Redesign and Recoding Report. Based on the data and insights that were thus unearthed, DISC composed a detailed Web Marketing Plan and proceeded on to an intensive SEO phase, fully optimizing a large number of key pages on the JA site, as well as a number of pages on JA's separate sister site, ASWE, DISC also "partially" optimized a batch

CASE STUDY: JERRYS ARTARAMA

of less-critical pages, focusing primarily on HTML titles, meta tags, headers, and footers. We also ensured that the site's code and navigation systems were optimally open to the search engine spiders and that the site smoothly circulated and amplified Google's "PageRank" factor — two crucial parts of successful SEO for large, dynamic Web sites.

For the PPC campaign, DISC adopted a two-prong strategy combining bulk submission of low-bid, low-management terms with semi-automatic bid management of more competitive phrases, starting with a list of 250 optimal phrases. To precisely track results, DISC relied on the GoToast (later called Atlas One Point) system, while also manually adjusted the bid prices as needed. Over the next several years, DISC has grown increasingly adept at manipulating bids to extract the best possible ROI and ROAS (return on ad spend) for JA. DISC applies multiple rules to the same ad to create complex bidding formulas that give a tremendous edge over competitors.

Another key element of the value DISC delivers is the detailed monthly PPC reports that describe what actions have been taken, and calculate the corresponding ROI and ROAS. These reports have generated great confidence on JA's part that its best interests are being served.

DISC has performed ongoing SEO for JA, totaling over 50 pages between their two sites. Of course, much less optimization work has been needed after doing it right the first time. Part of the beauty of SEO is that doing it well frees up a client to focus resources on other Web marketing.

In addition to SEO, PPC, and trusted feed, DISC has performed most of the other Web marketing activities that JA has needed over the years. This includes a highly detailed usability study that prompted JA to revamp its sub-par site-search module as well as make many adjustments and changes to "tweak" the site towards perfection. It also includes shopping-site marketing, Internet yellow pages, occasional copy writing, and research in unique problems and opportunities. Each year DISC prepares an omnibus Web Marketing Report and Plan for JA that details the previous year's work and ROI and previews the year ahead.

DISC's contract with JA consists mainly of a monthly retainer divided into tasks (SEO, PPC, etc.). We also quote one-time jobs as needed during the year. At the beginning of the year, we agree to a total budget, including DISC's labor and all click charges. In 2006, DISC will come under budget by about $100,000, while accomplishing all tasks and earning maximum ROI.

Results

The JA site saw a massive increase in organic referrals immediately following DISC's

CASE STUDY: JERRYS ARTARAMA

SEO work. As the number of pages indexed by Google went from dozens to thousands, referrals more than quadrupled, and many search terms rocketed to first place positions in the engines.

JA also saw a correspondingly huge increase in sales. One month after DISC performed SEO on the site at the end of 2003, sales rose by more than 50%, and from December 2003 to December 2004, sales more than doubled.

The PPC campaign got off to a good start, though it could hardly be expected to yield the same astonishing results as the first wave of SEO. In the first year alone, gross profits from PPC were approximately $70k, or $140k when calculated with "repeat viral" sales included. From the beginning, DISC has paid ultra-close attention to the ROI for each and every term used in PPC, and this strategy has also driven strong profits. Finally, in the first year the total ROI for DISC's activities for JA came to roughly $2 million, and more like $3.5 million when repeat viral is factored in. These are truly incredible results on an investment of less than $50k.

Results into 2005 and 2006 continued to be spectacular, with about 100,000 additional visitors per month in 2005. With a conversion rate of about 2%, this was nothing less than a windfall. Gross profit from PPC was three times the amount of the previous year, and DISC's trusted feed campaign yielded superb results: $600k revenues on $43.5k costs. The gross profit from trusted feed was actually higher than that from PPC. Trusted feed has many advantages: low click charges, highly specific ads, high conversion rates (4.5% for JA in December 2005), and relatively low management requirements.

About DISC:

DISC, at **www.2disc.com**, has been doing search engine marketing (SEO, PPC, trusted feeds, shopping site marketing, IYP, and ROI tracking) continuously since 1997. It serves all kinds of companies, large and small, in a broad range of business areas. The firm has extensive proof of success, as the references on its long client page will attest. DISC's employees, highly educated and long seasoned in SEM, all do thorough and continuous research to back DISC's methods and to educate clients. The company is also highly proficient in Web design and all Web and database programming, so it can integrate SEM into any kind of site. DISC is thoroughly versed in usability design for conversion rate optimization, so its SEM produces maximum profit, and the firm focuses intensely on clients' ROI, from the proposal stage to reporting.

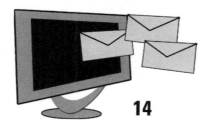

14

HINTS, TIPS, & ADVICE FROM THE EXPERTS WHO DO IT EVERYDAY

Pay-Per-Click Advice from WisdomClicks

By Mariano Katz

Let's agree on one thing: Working the numbers to create and optimize an effective pay-per-click (PPC) campaign is very important. We assign numbers to a budget, assign numbers on a maximum price per click per keyword, numbers for a top position for the ad, numbers to monitor and improve the number of clicks, the click through rate, numbers on the spending and the Return of Investment, numbers, numbers, numbers.

Managing so many figures and statistics makes us lose sight of something advertisers cannot live without: the Message, both in the ad and the Web site.

e-marketing offers the opportunity that no other medium has before: To compete side by side with top businesses, even if yours is in its infancy and your office is the breakfast table with a laptop on it.

Through e-marketing, any business will have the opportunity, even with a small budget, to be seen next to any giant competitor that allocates 60 advertisers and two floors of their crystal skyscraper to compete against you.

The following scenario is my own experience, and can exemplify what I just said:

Pay-Per-Click Advice from WisdomClicks

My firm manages the e-marketing campaigns for a franchised hotel in Florida; let's call it "Great Hotel of Florida." This franchised hotel is independently owned and operated, and their PPC budget is only $700 a month. After running a successful campaign for a couple of months, the hotel received notification from their franchise, let's call it "Great Hotels International," expressing their dissatisfaction that the hotel's e-marketing campaign was outranking the franchisor's e-marketing campaign for that particular area. Not only was the hotel running a better campaign than their competitors in the area, it was doing a better job than their multibillion dollar franchisor.

So now you have the opportunity to be seen. The question is, "How do you want to be seen?" And we get back to the Message.

The following tips help deliver the Message, more effectively. These tips are not new, they are way older than the Internet, and have been used for decades in all sorts of successful campaigns. In no way am I taking credit for them. The purpose of this article is to remind you that you should use them more than ever because you are visible and competing in the major leagues.

Customers don't look for the best price; they look for the best VALUE. That means getting the most for the same price.

Don't offer cheaper prices; offer more value. Not only will you be able to charge more, customers will perceive your company at higher standards.

Your ad and your Web site need to anticipate your prospects and offer a solution for those needs.

"We offer Airport Shuttle / Free Hot Breakfast / Free Wi-Fi" instead of "The best hotel in Florida at the best price."

Instead of describing how luxurious your products and/or services are, you should focus on describing how they benefit your prospects.

"Get a restful night in our new firm mattresses" as opposed to "Our new beds are top of the line!"

Encourage your prospects to take action.

"Book 3 nights and enjoy a 20% discount" will be more effective than "The cheapest hotel in the city."

Bill Gates once expressed the idea that the Internet is the most democratic medium because everyone has a chance to be part of if, as opposed to expensive and exclusive TV and print ads.

Pay-Per-Click Advice from WisdomClicks

I happen to agree, so... let's show the best of us.

Mariano Katz

Founder of WisdomClicks

www.wisdomclicks.com

As it happens to many people, sometimes the combination of two professional backgrounds results in a brand new profession. In my early twenties I was a computer programmer, and a few years later I graduated in Hospitality Management. The need to promote my hotel in the e-marketing era made me explore this field.

For the last five years my firm has been creating hundreds of PPC campaigns for companies in many different fields at a great success rate.

The 5 Easiest Ways to Increase ROI and Generate Qualified Leads Through Google PPC Advertising

By Hollis Thomases

1. Don't Settle for #1 — Many Google PPC advertisers feel that if their ads are #1 then their PPC campaign is successful. From our experience running PPC campaigns for several national and Fortune 1000 companies, we can tell you that the #1 position isn't always the best for all situations. Our advice: Spend the time to properly set up a Web site to track conversions and cost-per-conversion (see below for how you can do that within Google AdWords) and watch the results carefully when you move your ad from #1 to #3 and #4 positions. It may be that your conversions aren't affected by position and you can save money while decreasing your cost-per-lead.

2. Are You Getting the Most From Your Campaign Set-Up? — Is your Google PPC campaign one long list of keywords? If so, you may not be getting the most out of your campaign set-up. Your campaign will benefit significantly from taking advantage of AdWords ability to set up multiple campaigns and multiple adgroups. Don't put all your eggs in one basket! Separate your keywords into smaller, more targeted adgroups with ad copy that is specific to those keywords, so that you can track the progress of your campaign on a granular level. Is this old news and you're ready to take it one step further? From our previous work with a leading technology and security company a PPC campaign divided into low and high performing keywords will allow you to make the most out of your PPC budget without sacrificing visibility and brand awareness for key terms.

3. Negative Keywords Boost Quality Clicks — Are you using negative keywords? If not, you're missing an opportunity to decrease the amount of "noise" in your

The 5 Easiest Ways to Increase ROI and Generate Qualified Leads Through Google PPC Advertising

campaign. For one of our technology clients, we found that a critical keyword for their campaign, "wireless security," was generating too many ad impressions and clicks from people who were searching for home security systems. After implementing negative keywords that remove our ad from search queries that also included home security terms, our conversion rate jumped and we saw a significant drop in our cost-per-conversion. With a very simple technique we were able to further target our PPC campaign to the kind of customers we wanted to reach.

4.   Google's Conversion Tracking Feature — The best way to understand how your PPC campaign is increasing leads and sales is to track conversions from your ads and keywords. These conversions may be a customer filling out a contact form, buying a product, or reaching a contact information page. While there are many third party software programs that allow you to set up conversion funnels and tracking for PPC campaigns, Google AdWords allows you set this up right within your AdWords campaign so that you can see keyword performance next to conversion percentage and cost-per-conversion data. With the Google Conversion feature in place, you have the data needed to see which keywords are performing and leading to conversions and which ones may just be wasting money.

5.   Ad Testing — Never EVER run only one ad for your PPC campaign! Google allows you to create up to 50 — yes 50! — ad variations that will be served in rotation. Try out every way to reach your customers and then see which ads bring in the most results.

Hollis Thomases founded Web Ad.vantage in 1998, when the Internet was in its infancy and most businesses were primarily focused on building Web sites. Realizing that "if we build it, they will come" was not enough, Thomases recognized the secret to success was in generating qualified Web site traffic and converting those leads into sales. She pioneered innovative programs that consistently enhanced her clients' image and bottom line, spearheading her agency's impressive growth well after the Internet boom and subsequent bust. Thomases is a noted industry spokeswoman and the sole recipient of the Baltimore District Office of the U.S. Small Business Administration's 2007 "Small Business Person of the Year" award for the state of Maryland.

Web Ad.vantage is a privately-held woman-owned agency. Its core competencies include online advertising, search engine optimization, paid search campaign management, and Internet strategy. The Web Ad.vantage client roster includes: Nokia USA, Zurich North America, Nature Made Vitamins, Johns Hopkins University, George Washington University, Long Fence and Long Home, Carapace, Pointsec, and Baltimore Area Convention and Visitors Association. The agency has been recognized by Smart Woman magazine as a "Best Place for Business Women to Work." Visit **www.webadvantage.net**

When Pay Per Click Doesn't Work

By Carla Hunnicutt

Pay-per-click (PPC) advertising is a great way to get fast, targeted traffic to your Web site; however, there are a few requirements that should be in place before launching an aggressive campaign. I also want to mention that I work for an interactive marketing agency based in Atlanta, Georgia that happens to do quite a bit of pay-per-click advertising for our clients. We're a Google Qualified company and it may come as a surprise that we actually discourage some firms from launching PPC campaigns.

Like any good marketing agency, we do not advocate initiatives that do not make sense. We can drive traffic to your site all day long, but if you're not getting enough sales or leads, then what's the point?

That being said, we have a simple formula that serves as a litmus test for determining if PPC is a worthy initiative for our perspective clients to undertake.

Good Landing Pages + Good Products + Targeted Traffic = Conversion.

Seems simple and it is. However, in a world of nuance many good firms can get off track. I will explore each of these a bit further below.

Good Landing Pages

Good landing pages encompass more than simply being visually appealing. Strong landing pages are based on clearly defined Web objectives that can be mapped back to clearly defined organizational objectives.

Each landing page should have a purpose and that purpose should be to drive the Web visitors to an action (online order, lead, phone call, etc.). By having a clearly defined strategy and objective, the creative process can begin.

Great creative isn't cheap or easy. But it's vital. To drive PPC traffic to a site or landing page with poor creative just isn't smart marketing. This often leads to the question of how to determine if the creative is good enough. This of course is never an easy answer, as opinions vary. However, data does not. The first place to look is at the conversion rate.

Conversion rates vary across industries, but if you're conversion rate is low the chances that driving additional traffic will create the impact you're looking for isn't very likely. Of course there could be targeting or product issues, and we will address those in a bit, but the odds are that if you don't convert the traffic you currently receive then you need to re-evaluate your Web site before a significant PPC campaign is launched.

When Pay Per Click Doesn't Work

Good Products

This of course is one of the most difficult conversations to have with prospective clients. Bad products don't sell well. They can be over-priced, under-priced, not up to the competition's specs, or simply past their prime. No matter how one looks at it, bad products are that — bad.

No amount of marketing can save a bad product. You can combine highly targeted Web site traffic with the right landing pages and the result over time will be failure if the products are inferior. As a marketing agency, we have had occasion to advise prospects to take their marketing dollars and re-invest them in product development and then come back to us.

Other quality interactive agencies have probably offered the same advice. Highly motivated and skilled PPC teams thrive on success. Bringing projects doomed to failure is in nobody's long-term interest. It tarnishes the company and the PPC agency, in addition to the enormous amount of cash burned.

Targeted Traffic

This is obviously where PPC advertising comes in. This is the easy part, so to speak. Google, Yahoo!, MSN, and others are getting better and better at delivering highly targeted Web traffic. When you mix good products and good landing pages with a good SEM firm that can provide extensive keyword and competitive research, proper campaign strategy and execution, geo-targeting, bid management, day parting and ad scheduling, compelling ad copy, ongoing PPC optimization and reporting, you can start to see the formula come together.

Conversion

Conversion is not an accident. Everyone knows this, but too many firms don't embrace this. Conversion is simply the combination of the right products coupled with right traffic and creative. It's that simple.

So, if your firm lacks good creative, then be wary of launching an aggressive PPC campaign until this is in place. If your firm lacks good products, do not pour money into PPC or any other marketing campaign without heavily re-investing in product development.

Conversion is what matters. PPC is not right for all firms. Good agencies want to work with clients that have products and services they believe in. Good agencies want to drive PPC traffic that leads to conversion. Good agencies believe that when you combine the right keywords with the right landing pages and the right products, good things happen.

When Pay Per Click Doesn't Work

Carla Hunnicutt is the Director of PPC Advertising at NeboWeb (www.NeboWeb.com).

As Director of PPC Advertising, Hunnicutt has led NeboWeb to tremendous growth in the area of search engine marketing. She provides brilliant pay-per-click strategies and extensive search marketing experience to NeboWeb. She has a Bachelor's Degree from the University of Georgia in Comparative Literature and is a Google AdWords Qualified Professional. Prior to joining NeboWeb, Hunnicutt was the former Director of Marketing for a prominent Atlanta-based company.

Google Tips

By Tony Tateossian

- Google PageRank works by pointing other into a particular page of your site. Tis will help boost your page rank at Google. Make sure the other sites have a good page rank; 5 and over is very good.

- When requesting links, use your keyword in the anchor text, meaning the hyperlink linking back to your site. This will help you rank higher for that keyword in Google. The more sites linking into your particular page with a specific keyword will help you rank higher, especially if those sites have a high Google page rank.

- Use Google Sitemaps to index your Web site properly. Create an XML site map for Google. Also create an HTML sitemap for other search engine crawlers.

- For Google AdWords pay-per click advertising, make sure your keywords are ones that would convert your traffic into sales. Test each keyword by tracking your campaign carefully and use Google Analytics. Also group your keywords into categories and then create proper landing pages pertaining to each category for highest possible conversions.

Cosmodex™ (www.cosmodex.com) was created for people who want to effectively promote their Web sites without spending huge amounts of money. When you join Cosmodex™, your site is indexed right away and immediately benefits with free, targeted traffic, points per click, core search results, highlighted listings, and cost per impression for positions 1, 2, and 3 — all free of cost. When you join Cosmodex™, we prove that it isn't necessary to spend a fortune to be in the top 20, top 10 . . . or top 5!

tony@cosmodex.com

www.Cosmodex.com

Four Tips to Increase Search Engine Rankings

By Scott Buresh

Most businesses don't take advantage of various techniques to increase search engine ranking, but few things on the Internet can be as beneficial as a high ranking on a search engine. A recent Forrester Research report showed that 80% of Web surfers discover the new sites that they visit through search engines (such as Yahoo, Google, or MSN). According to iProspect, 85% of Web users use search engines to find solutions and vendors. Properly optimizing a site to increase your search engine ranking for each page helps it to attract numerous, highly targeted visitors — visitors that may become buyers.

For the technically inclined, there are numerous places on the Web to get detailed, in-depth information on how to achieve a high ranking on a search engine. However, many people don't care about the technical aspects of search engine optimization — they just want to know what is wrong with their site (and how to fix it). What follows is a practical guide that covers some of the most basic tips that can be used to increase search engine ranking. It is in no way intended to be comprehensive, but it should help the average site owner determine whether their site is optimized, and if not, how to make some simple changes to give each individual page of their site a better chance for a high ranking on a search engine.

Issue #1 - The Title Bar

This is one of the most often overlooked techniques to increase search engine ranking. On your homepage, what does the title bar say? If you use Internet Explorer, this is the blue bar at the very top of the window that displays your page (it may include the words "Microsoft Internet Explorer" at the end). Does your company name appear here by itself when you have more important keywords to emphasize? Worse yet, does it say "untitled"? If you want to increase the search engine ranking for that page, this area should contain the most important keywords you see on your homepage. To check the rest of your site, click on any link from your homepage and see if the words in this title bar change for each page in your site. They should — and each title bar should contain the most important keywords from its corresponding page. Note: Very long keyword strings in the title bar should be avoided — six words or less is optimal. Also, words in the title bar should not repeat more than once, and identical words should not appear next to one another.

Issue #2 - Content

Search engines all try to list sites that contain good content. Translation: You need words on your pages to achieve a high ranking on a search engine, not flashy graphics. This text should contain the most important keywords that your potential customers would use to find you on a search engine. If you have very few or no words on a page where you wish to increase the search engine ranking, it is a good idea to add some

Four Tips to Increase Search Engine Rankings

where you wish to increase the search engine ranking, it is a good idea to add some, ideally around 250 per page. For aesthetic reasons, this is not always practical, but even 100 well-written words will give you a better opportunity for a high ranking on a search engine than none. It is also important that you make certain that the words are written in a language the search engines can read. Using your mouse, bring your cursor down to the text on one of your Web pages. Clicking and holding down the left mouse button (make sure you aren't near a link) see if you can highlight just one or two words of the text. If you can, everything is most likely fine. If nothing happens, or you can only highlight a large block, it is most likely in graphic form. To increase search engine ranking in such cases, the graphic text needs to be replaced by standard HTML text to allow the search engines to read it. Your Web expert should have no problem understanding what you require, and the transition should be fairly simple and affordable.

Issue #3 - Meta Tags

Some people believe that meta tags are the Holy Grail of achieving a high ranking on a search engine. Unfortunately, their effectiveness is limited (many engines ignore them completely), but they can play a limited role on some engines. To see if your site has meta tags, go to your home page. Click the "view" command at the top of the browser window. From the pull-down menu, select "source." This should open up another window that shows your code. Much of this may seem indecipherable, but there should be two commands there (usually near the top of the code). One of these says meta name="description" content= and will go on to describe your company and products, and one says meta name="keywords" content= and goes on to list applicable keywords for your site. If these tags are missing, have your Web expert insert them. Again, this may not do much to increase search engine ranking, but it will not hurt.

Issue #4 - Links

Link popularity has become increasingly important for those who wish to increase search engine ranking, with 19 of the top 20 engines using it in their ranking algorithms. Simply put, search engines give a ranking boost to sites that have links from quality, related sites. There are numerous free tools on the Web that will allow you to see what sites link to yours (just type "free link popularity check" in your favorite search engine). If you don't have many sites linking to yours, it may be time to start a link building campaign. This is where you find quality, non-competing sites in your industry and ask them to link to your site. An additional benefit of link building is that these links can bring you additional, highly targeted traffic.

Conclusion

Although following the above guidelines will by no means guarantee you a high ranking

Four Tips to Increase Search Engine Rankings

on a search engine, fixing one or more of the problems should help increase your search engine ranking. For the volumes of potential customers that a search engine can send to your site, it's certainly worth the effort.

Scott Buresh, Chief Executive Officer
Medium Blue Search Engine Marketing
www.mediumblue.com

Scott Buresh is an internationally recognized authority on search engine marketing. His articles on the SEM industry have been translated into eight languages and have appeared in numerous influential industry publications, including ZDNet, WebProNews, MarketingProfs, DarwinMag, SiteProNews, SEO Today, ISEDB. com, and Search Engine Guide. He was also a contributor to the recently released Building Your Business with Google For Dummies (Wiley, 2004), and has been cited in several national publications, including B2B Magazine, Print Solutions, and The Hosting Standard. In 2001, Scott co-founded the Search Engine Consortium of Atlanta (SECA), a leading SEM organization (affiliated with the Atlanta Interactive Marketing Association) that is dedicated to promoting the discipline of search engine marketing in the city of Atlanta and beyond.

Pay-Per-Click Campaigns

By Tammy Schultz

Many people I talk to say they tried PPC but found it cost them too much money and had little response. What I have found is the number one reason for this is that they tried to go after the most generic term they could. Not only do these tend to be very expensive, but you will get lots of traffic that is not interested in buying your products.

You want to spend time thinking about and researching the terms you want to use. You also need to know what your monthly budget will be. Once you know that you can decide if you want to go after one or two of the generic terms in your industry or focus more on many terms that are less popular or more targeted.

For example — Let's say you manufacture wheelchair lift ramps. Your first thought might be to bid on "wheelchair," which had 124,714 searches done in August 2006 and is currently going for a bid amount of $1.60 to be number one. This would generate a lot of traffic but would also cost quite a bit of money. Instead look to terms that include the words "ramp" or "lift," such as "wheelchair lift ramp" that had 1,674 searches done in August 2006 and is currently going for a bid amount of $2.00. Sure it is more per click, but those 1,674 searches were of what you sell. This, in theory, will increase the number of sales, decreasing your return on investment.

Pay-Per-Click Campaigns

Don't forget about local searches. If you do business in a certain location then use the local searches that are offered. This can be done in a couple of ways. I recommend doing both. Both Yahoo and Google offer you the ability to have people within a certain mile radius see your ad when they search for something. Let's say you are selling a fitness franchise but only want to sell to people looking to start a business in the Chicago area. You would then create an account and have "fitness franchise" as one of your search terms and select a 50-mile radius around an address in Chicago. The other way to do a local search is to add the area to your search term. For example, if you are a carpet cleaner in Rochester, New York, one of your terms might be "carpet cleaner Rochester."

Once you have your search terms and your budget figured out, it is now time to write the ads. I find that by focusing each ad specifically to that search term I get a better result. I like to have the title match the search term exactly and then the description repeat. The description should read like a classified ad and generate excitement. Make searchers want to click on your link and not your competitors' links.

Unless your objective is branding, don't focus on getting the most traffic to your site; focus on getting quality traffic to your site.

www.virtualtech.com

Tammy Schultz is president of Virtualtech Web Site Design and Promotion, Inc. Tammy started Virtualtech in January of 1997 when she saw that small- to medium-size companies didn't know how to effectively market their products and services on the Web.

Tammy has been instrumental in establishing Virtualtech as a rising star among Web site marketing firms throughout the United States because of her approach of looking at her clients' Web sites from the visitor's point of view. Tammy's ability to explain all that is involved in creating and marketing a Web site, in terms that people understand, has been another driving force to Virtualtech's success.

Tammy is a professional speaker and author and has hosted a number of cable television and radio shows. Her four-step program, Elements of an Effective Web site, explains the steps in creating and marketing a Web site, has been featured on the SCORE and Business Professional Women's Web sites, and for several seminars for Chambers of Commerce, SCORE, Wisconsin Women's Business Initiative Corporation (WWBIC), Concordia University, and others.

Google TrustRank

By Paul Bliss

There has been an ever increasing awareness to the value of Google's "TrustRank" algorithm. While there are many factors that are "Off-page," there are a number of simple actions you can take to make sure your site earns the trust from Google by employing these easy techniques.

The best way to think about TrustRank is to compare it to if you were to purchase a product or service in the real world. There are many built-in factors that we use to pre-qualify a business to see if we are willing to part with our cash for their goods or services. This is the same approach Google takes in order to measure the quality of a site, and doing this will get you out of the so-called "sandbox" much faster than the typical 4 to 6 months.

While in no particular order, some of these ideas are more costly than others, but all are worth doing.

- Register your domain for 10 years. If you can't afford the $70 it costs at GoDaddy, then are you really serious about your site?

- Buy a SSL certificate — this tells Google that you are a legit business since they know you have to have a verified checking account to get a SSL cert. (Buy it for as many years as you can at a time, at the very least for 2 years.).

- Have a privacy policy that tells in exact detail what happens to the information about the visitor that is collected from the site.

- List a mailing address (no P.O. Boxes) — Just as in real life, you feel better purchasing a service or product from a place that has a physical location.

- List your contact information — Telephone, fax (if needed), e-mail and name.

- If you have a bigger budget, use any of the "Hacker Safe" services and place those icons on your site. Again, this tells Google that you are seriously committed to protecting your visitor's experience on the site.

Those are simple techniques that you can directly apply to your site and are signals to Google that you take your online presence seriously.

As far as the "Off-page" factors, it's really about linking to quality sites that are relevant and sometimes considered "authority sites" by Google. Also, getting links from those trusted sites will help re-enforce the quality of your site in the eyes of the Google spiders.

Google TrustRank

Paul Bliss
www.SEOforGoogle.com

Paul Bliss has been optimizing sites for over seven years and has successfully ranked over 80 clients into top ranked positions on Google. He is a Certified eMarketer and is the author of the ebook SEO for Google, *which explains how to get your site top rankings in Google.*

How Google Indexes Your Site

By Paul Bliss

I can't tell you how many times I've answered this question in forums, so I figured since so many are asking, it would make for a great article.

First off, let's describe what we are talking about. A "bot" is a piece of software from a search engine that is built to go through every page of your site, categorize it, and place it into a database.

Google has three well known bots: The AdSense bot, the Freshbot, and the DeepCrawl.

The AdSense bot, as you could probably guess, is used for publishers who have AdSense on their sites. As soon as a new page is created, the JavaScript within the AdSense code sends a message to the AdSense bot, and it will come within 15 minutes to index the page so that it can serve up the most relevant ads.

But for this conversation we are only concerned about the DeepCrawl and the Freshbot.

The Freshbot crawls the most popular pages on your Web site. It doesn't matter if that is one page or thousands. Sites like Amazon.com and CNN.com have pages that are crawled every ten minutes, since Google has learned that those pages have that amount of frequent changes. A typical site should expect to have a Freshbot visit every 1 to 14 days, depending on how popular those pages are.

What happens to your site on a Freshbot visit is that it finds all of the deeper links in your site. It places those links into a database so that when the DeepCrawl occurs, it has a reference.

How Google Indexes Your Site

Once a month, the DeepCrawl bot visits your site and goes over all the links found by the Freshbot. This is the reason why it can take up to a month for your entire site to be indexed in Google — even with the addition of a Google Sitemap.

So, be patient and keep on adding content to your site, and work on getting valuable in-bound links to your site — Google will reward you for it.

Paul Bliss
www.SEOforGoogle.com

Paul Bliss has been optimizing sites for over seven years and has successfully ranked over 80 clients into top ranked positions on Google. He is a Certified eMarketer and is the author of the ebook SEO for Google, *which explains how to get your site top rankings in Google.*

Search Engine Optimization for Google

By Paul Bliss

With the recent Jagger update settling, many people find their sites no longer have the high rankings they had for so long enjoyed prior to the latest Google update.

So, the sites that lost these rankings are scrambling to find some answers as to why their site dropped. While it's my business to know the intricacies of how this particular update impacted the search algorithm, there are some common ground starting points that if you apply these to all of your sites, you should be able to survive any update intact.

- Proper naming structure

- Name your page titles with your keywords if possible

- Always have a sitemap

- Always include a robots.txt file

- Don't use hidden text

- Make sure your keyword phrase is included in your H1 tags

- Don't optimize for more than two keywords per page

- Use text links where possible

- Offload all your js and css code

Search Engine Optimization for Google

- In any product image, be sure to use the alt tag

- Use hyphens, not underscores when you name a page file

- Make sure your site has an error handling page

- Create a Google Sitemap and submit it to them (This is in addition to a typical sitemap)

- Don't forget about meta tags

- If you must use a re-direct, be sure it's server side, not with a meta refresh tag

Be sure to follow these simple guidelines and you won't need to worry too much anytime Google has an update — your site will not be impacted by any filters that are checking for spamming, hidden text, or anything that resembles cloaking.

Paul Bliss
www.SEOforGoogle.com

Paul Bliss has been optimizing sites for over seven years and has successfully ranked over 80 clients into top ranked positions on Google. He is a Certified eMarketer and is the author of the ebook SEO for Google, *which explains how to get your site top rankings in Google.*

How to Get Your Site a Top Ranking in Google

By Paul Bliss

It's the new American dream. Your Web site appears in a top spot on Google for your chosen keyword. Next thing you know, orders start coming in faster than you can handle, and you are rolling in the money. If only it were so easy, right?

Well, it can be done. I've done it many times in many different industries. There is no secret, but rather it's just knowing what to do. I've made just about every mistake one can make with a Web site, but I learned from every setback. If you were only allowed to do one thing to get ranked for your site in Google, without a doubt, all you'd need to do is get links for your site.

Yes, there are many other factors involved in getting your site to a top position. But this is the most powerful way as of this writing to get a top spot in Google. It's not just enough to have links pointing to your site, but you need to have your keyword

How to Get Your Site a Top Ranking in Google

"anchor linked" to your site. Anchor linking is when you use your keyword phrase as the click-able text for a link. So, instead of saying "Click Here", you would use "Widgets" as the link text.

Now, another point of consideration is determining what keyword/phrase you want to use to get your site found. Most times, people impulsively choose a one word phrase. While this would be a great way to bring traffic to your site, would it bring targeted traffic, with people looking specifically for your product or service? Most times when people type in a one letter key phrase, they are in the beginning of their search.

They may type in "Shoes," but are really looking for "Running Shoes." So, if you have a top ranking for shoes, do you serve that user's needs? Maybe, but they may also be looking for dress, casual, women's, men's, children's, athletic, girl's, boy's, etc. This is why when you begin to optimize your site, you should focus on more targeted keyword phrases.

Suppose you sell a certain brand name of dress shoes. For this example, we'll call the famous brand XYZ. So, by getting anchor links as "XYZ Dress Shoes," you are already eliminating those users who are looking for another brand or line of shoe. Next, you need to make sure that the page that gets linked contains the on the page content with "XYZ Dress Shoes." If you would link to a page without relevant content, Google would view this link as possible spam, or more appropriately, irrelevant content.

Now, once you have compiled your list of keywords, you need to see which ones are searched on the most. The best tool for this is WordTracker, and it is worth the tiny fee you need to pay to have access for one day. There are also free tools online that you can use, but WordTracker will give you the most accurate results.

Once you have run through your list of all your keywords, the obvious choice is to pick the ones with the highest amount of searches (and content relevant to your site!). The next step is to then begin the process of a link campaign. Now, I can already hear you complaining about doing a link exchange. This is only 1/3 of your campaign. The ideal method is to not only engage in a reciprocal link exchange, but to also engage in strategic linking.

Strategic linking is when you get a link to your site without having to return the favor. What's the best way to do this? Write an article just like this one. If I get one Web site to use this article and have it point to my site, I've just created another link to my site. Pretty easy, eh?

Since you have now engaged in a linking campaign, you should expect to see results in Google in as little as 4 days, and as far as 6 months. All of this is determined by

How to Get Your Site a Top Ranking in Google

where your links are coming from, and the popularity of the site from which the link came. Next, you need to get as many links as you can pointing to your site with your popular keyword phrase anchor linked to your site.

As I mentioned before, there are many other factors that will only enhance your rankings in Google, but the implementation of a link campaign is the strongest method to get your site to a top ranking!

Paul Bliss
www.SEOforGoogle.com

Paul Bliss has been optimizing sites for over seven years and has successfully ranked over 80 clients into top ranked positions on Google. He is a Certified eMarketer and is the author of the ebook SEO for Google, *which explains how to get your site top rankings in Google.*

Why Your Google Campaign Isn't Working and What to Do About It

By Eric Layland

In order to address what it means to fail at search advertising, we first need to define success.

Many business-to-business (B2B) marketers fail in searches without even knowing it. The very basic performance reports available through Google™ and other search providers can lead an advertiser to believe that his or her campaign is generating plenty of qualified interest, when the actual truth could be precisely the opposite.

Search success is not defined by impressions, clicks, or even cost per click. Certainly, you could argue that a high number of impressions means that many people are seeing your ad, but even that can be misleading. "Impressions" is simply a count of the number of times your ad is served. Whether people are actually paying attention is a different matter.

Clicks, click-through rate (CTR), and cost-per-click (CPC) are the measuring sticks of most search campaigns, primarily because they're the statistics most easily gleaned from online reports. As this paper discusses (see page 4), judging a campaign's performance by these standards is not only misleading, it can cause an advertiser to waste significant investment.

Why? Because a click is only one action — it doesn't measure what that prospect did when he or she clicked on your ad (i.e., did he or she become e a lead or buy your

Why Your Google Campaign Isn't Working and What to Do About It

product), or even how qualified he or she is. Our experience tells us that many advertisers are content to generate thousands of clicks at considerable cost, but on further analysis, discover that the vast majority of those clicks are completely worthless.

The perfect search campaign is one that:

- Generates a Cost Per Acquisition (CPA) — whether your "acquisition" is a lead, download, registration, or sale — competitive with other advertising vehicles

- Generates predictable results (measured by CPA) at projected spend levels

- Is sufficiently expansive to cover every keyword or phase, and every variation of those words or phrases, that a qualified prospect would conceivably search on

- Is designed to deliver relevant ad copy for every keyword (to drive clicks) and mapped to relevant landing pages (to drive conversions)

- Is designed in such a way that specific terms, groups of terms, and campaigns are all optimized separately, with separate budgets, ad copy, geo-targeting, and day-parting

- Is tracked through use of a back-end database or CRM system that measures ROI on a keyword-by-keyword basis

Don't have all these metrics in place? Don't worry — no-one does. The scenario above is the ideal program, and a hypothetical ideal at that. But that doesn't mean that you shouldn't use these standards as goals to strive for, and as benchmarks for your current program.

Successful search advertising is complicated. Search programs are easy to set up, but much more difficult to manage, optimize, and otherwise refine into a successful campaign. Doing so takes time, effort, resources, dedication, and investment.

This paper is designed to point you in the right direction.

Mistake #1: Not Tracking Desired Actions

The lack of an appropriate and complete tracking system is one of the most common errors, or omissions, that advertisers make in setting up a paid serach program.

It's easy to see why. Google provides basic tracking services — impressions, clicks, cost per click — automatically and at no charge as part of the default set-up. Going beyond that basic set-up, a critical step in being able to gauge the true success of

Why Your Google Campaign Isn't Working and What to Do About It

any search campaign, requires a modest investment in time and resources that most companies figure they can live without.

The foundation of a strong search campaign is knowing what you want to achieve. Are you trying to generate downloads, registrations, page views, sales leads, qualified leads, sales? How are you defining that goal: Is someone filling out a registration form, hitting a particular page, meeting certain qualification criteria? Your search campaign should measure:

1. How many of those desired actions are taking place

2. How much each desired action is costing in the aggregate, and

3. Which precise keywords are generating those actions at the lowest cost.

Keep in mind that you may have separate goals for certain parts of the program. For example, you may wish to measure the performance of "branded terms" — the name of your company, product names, names of competitors — based on impressions, or even ad position, whereas more generic terms will be measured on Cost Per Lead or Cost Per Qualified Lead.

Clicks	CTR	Avg CPC	Cost	Avg Position	Conversions ▲	Conversion Rate	Cost / Conversion
650	0.32%	$1.95	$1,267.35	3.6	74	11.40%	$17.07
293	0.35%	$1.67	$490.42	2.1	67	22.87%	$7.32
282	4.40%	$1.52	$429.44	1.7	61	21.79%	$6.93
98	5.30%	$1.93	$189.47	1.4	27	27.84%	$6.96
62	3.58%	$1.83	$113.58	1.6	13	20.97%	$8.74
12	2.40%	$1.87	$22.44	2.8	3	25.00%	$7.48
19	2.28%	$3.05	$57.93	3.3	3	15.79%	$19.31

Fig. 1. Only by tracking desired actions, in this case sales leads, can a search advertiser accurately gauge the success of their program, and optimize it accordingly.

Your tracking system can never be good enough. Don't stop tracking at clicks, because you'll have no idea how those clicks are converting into leads. Don't stop tracking at leads, because you'll have no idea how many of those leads are qualified, or which are converting into sales. Don't stop tracking at sales, because you'll have no idea how those sales are retaining or generating additional lifetime value. And so on.

Most advertisers only measure clicks and cost-per-click for reasons stated above. To the novice search marketer, seeing the number of clicks generated by your efforts can be rewarding, but they are only part of the story. In fact, simply knowing which terms are generating the most clicks or the lowest cost-per-click is generally worthless.

Why Your Google Campaign Isn't Working and What to Do About It

That's because the keywords that generate the most clicks are very often simply more generic terms that attract a wider spectrum of prospects. Likewise, terms that generate clicks at a low cost could be converting to leads (or sales) at a low rate, while other terms that generate clicks at a slightly higher cost could actually be your best performers.

At a bare minimum, we always recommend implementing some kind of conversion tracking so you'll know which terms are generating actual leads or registrations. By tracking conversions to the keyword, you'll be able to optimize your bid strategy and overall media spend. You'll understand which keywords are responsible for driving desired actions, as well as which terms only drive costs without the desired pay-off.

Google offers a free conversion tracking service through its AdWords program. (Yahoo! and MSN offer similar programs.) The Google system involves placing a cookie on a user's computer when he or she clicks on an ad, so that if the user clicks on your ad and then reaches one of your conversion pages (for example, the "thank you" page that appears after submitting a registration form), the user's browser sends the cookie to a Google server, and Google records a successful conversion. More sophisticated programs may benefit from third-party tracking solutions.

If branding or awareness is your primary goal, your campaign can still benefit from tracking. Simply tracking click-throughs and site visits is only a basic measurement. If your ultimate goal is to engage those visitors, page views, and time spent on the site are helpful benchmarks that can help more precisely measure the value of each visit. Web analytics tools, such as Google Analytics, can provide you this additional insight.

Here are two important facts to understand and keep in mind when setting up and designing your search program:

- You get paid on acquiring new customers.

- Google gets paid on clicks.

Google and other search engines don't care much if you get customers or not. They just want you to keep feeding the meter. Search engines earn revenue for each click regardless whether the visitor was looking for "enterprise expense management services" or "Starship Enterprise." When you have a tracking system that takes advantage of all the data available, you'll begin to realize the value and power of search marketing.

Mistake #2: Poor Program Architecture

A Google account is comprised of three levels: campaigns, ad groups, and keywords.

Why Your Google Campaign Isn't Working and What to Do About It

A standard account can have up to 25 campaigns, each of which can include 100 ad groups. Most novice search marketers, constrained by time, budget, or resources, set up their Google programs in a very simple form: one monolithic campaign with a handful of ad groups.

The result is a program doomed to perform far below its potential.

Campaigns can be used in a variety of ways, but it's critically important that the ad groups within each campaign are related in some way. Campaigns can be used to target certain markets, organize product/service lines, group like-behaving keywords, or for any other purpose that simplifies program management and optimizes overall performance.

The vast majority of search marketers place all their ad groups in one campaign. This is a common mistake that results in a program that will never be fully optimized because the campaign level is where you control budget, day-parting, geo-targeting, etc. A good example of this is where a daily budget is exhausted by the end of the business day, say, on the West Coast. The solution is to set up two campaigns — one for each territory — and assign a separate budget to each, each budget dedicated to ensuring ads appear throughout the business day in that particular time zone.

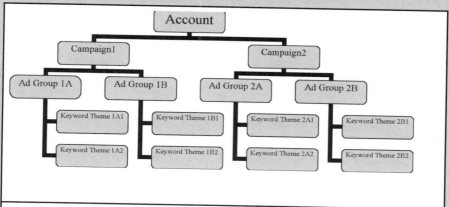

Fig. 2. The chart provides an example of the relationships between organization levels of a Google account. Note that each should be distinct from other groupings. The architecture is defined by overall campaign goals and objectives.

Ad groups contain groups of keywords. At a very basic level, keywords within each ad group should be similar in concept or topic; for example, all keywords related to "performance," or "cost savings" or a particular product or industry. If keywords reflecting a wide range of topics are all contained within the same ad group, the ad copy will need to be generic enough to address that same range of topics; therefore,

Why Your Google Campaign Isn't Working and What to Do About It

it will be largely irrelevant to some subset of those keywords. Conversely, the greater the number of ad groups, the more the ad copy can be precisely relevant to each particular topic or product or message. The result: much higher click-through and conversion (click-to-lead) rates.

Mistake #3: Not Using Custom Microsites or Landing Pages

Most novice search marketers direct traffic from search ads to either their corporate home page, a just-barely-relevant product page or a generic landing page (one that was originally designed to capture registrations from random visitors to the corporate site).

These and other search campaigns like them often fail not because of keyword selection or ad copy, but on where traffic is directed from those ads. It's easy to understand the motivations behind wanting to leverage the investment already sunk into a corporate Web site by using it for search purposes, but doing so is a big mistake.

Remember, conversion rate — the rate at which clicks convert to leads or registrations — is as important as click rate in driving Cost Per Lead or Cost Per Acquisition. Double your conversion rate, for example, and you'll make an equivalent impact on the number of leads, and Cost Per Lead, as if you had doubled your click-through rate.

Corporate Web sites don't work as destination pages for search advertising largely because:

1. They present too many options, and

2. They're not directly relevant to the precise term or topic being searched.

A search campaign, as already discussed, is designed to drive a specific, desired action. The typical navigation bar that appears on most Web sites, however, means that a visitor arriving at any page on that site is presented with a myriad of links and other options. (Indeed, it's the very purpose of a well-designed Web site to make it easy for a visitor to jump from one section to another.) Most visitors who are dumped onto any page from a corporate site will therefore likely explore around the site and then disappear.

A well-designed microsite or custom landing page, however, is designed specifically to drive the desired action. The offer is strongly merchandised, extraneous navigation and other distractions are eliminated, and every ounce of copy is tailored to driving registration or whatever the desired action happens to be.

Why Your Google Campaign Isn't Working and What to Do About It

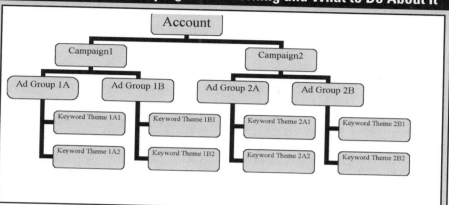

Fig. 3. Microsites serve as effective destinations for search programs because they present additional selling information to those prospects who need it, without forcing other prospects to wade through that information before filling out the registration form.

For purposes of this discussion, by "microsite" we mean a two-page or three-page custom mini-site (see Fig. 3) that combines a registration page with one or two peripheral pages that provide additional selling information. The concept behind this model is to present the registration form front and center for those prospects who are ready to submit their information immediately, yet provide the option for other prospects to learn a little more about the company, product, or offer, before they complete the form.

We generally prefer microsites to single landing pages because prospects responding to search advertising receive very little information on the front end (in the ad), and thus may require additional selling. This is markedly different from an e-mail campaign, for example, where the prospect may have already received a critical mass of information and be ready to register immediately. In our experience, microsites generate conversion rates up to 50 percent higher when tested against landing pages using the same offer.

Microsites and landing pages also perform better than corporate Web sites because the language and content can be customized to be more directly relevant to both the search term and the ad copy. In fact, the most successful search campaigns use not just one universal microsite, but multiple versions of that microsite, with copy and offer adjusted to increase the relevancy to a particular campaign, ad group, or even individual search term.

Relevancy is a key factor in search advertising success (see also our discussion of ad copy on page 11). Successful search marketers strive to maintain consistency and continuity through keywords, ad copy, and the microsite. A campaign that doesn't

Why Your Google Campaign Isn't Working and What to Do About It

acheive that consistency will fail, for example, when a prospect looking for "New Zealand air fare" sees an ad that says "New Zealand" and a landing page or microsite that says "New Zealand Cruises." Close, but not close enough.

Microsites are also fertile ground for testing. It's possible to substantially increase conversion rates over time by conducting so-called "A/B" tests of different headlines, offers, even design elements. In this manner, microsites can be optimized just like keywords and ad copy. Furthermore, testing microsites is more efficient, because once you have the person at the registration form, you can more easily control the variables in play, whereas with ad copy and keywords, you're competing with other paid and organic listings that may change from day to day.

Mistake #4: Over-Reliance on Google Broad Matching

Like many of the pitfalls described in this paper, overuse of the broad match type is related directly to default Google settings, and to the fact that most marketers simply don't invest the time or resources to extend their program beyond the most basic infrastructure.

Using broad match by default across all (or even most) of the keywords in your search program is a common mistake. It directly leads to overspending, because it generates unqualified clicks — clicks derived from prospects who aren't really searching for terms related directly to your product or service, but who saw (and clicked on) your ad anyway.

With broad match, nearly any search query can trigger your ad as long as your search term is included. For instance, if the term you register is "network software," even someone searching for "social network for software developers" would see your ad. Conversely, the more specific your keywords, the more qualified the resulting traffic, and the less money you'll waste on people whom you never intended to see your ad in the first place.

Let's review your options when it comes to match types:

Broad match is Google's default option. If you include general keyword or keyword phrases — for example, network software — in your keyword list, your ads will appear when a user's query contains "network" and "software" in any order, and may include other terms that are completely irrelevant to your specific product or service.

Using broad match, your ads will also automatically show for expanded matches. These include plural forms and what Google determines are relevant variations that may not be as relevant for you. When using broad match, consider restricting its use to keyword phrases with at least two words. Single term broad match keywords are

Why Your Google Campaign Isn't Working and What to Do About It

requently less targeted and can drive your cost excessively with little return to show for it.

Using the phrase match option, if you enter your keyword surrounded by quotation marks, such as "network software," your ad will appear when a user searches only on the phrase "network software," with the words in that order. Other terms can be included in the search but they must fall before or after your root keyword. For example, your ad would be triggered for the query "open source network software" but not for "network monitoring software." Targeting with phrase matching is more precise than broad matching and more flexible than the exact match option.

By surrounding your keywords with brackets (for example: [network software]) your ads will appear only when users search for the specific phrase: "network software." This option is called exact match. The query must be in this order and not contain any other terms. For instance, your ad will not display for a query on "networking software" or "enterprise network software." Exact matching is the most precise option and typically generates the least amount of traffic. Although your ads won't receive as many impressions, the benefit is that the clicks you do receive should convert to leads at a much higher rate.

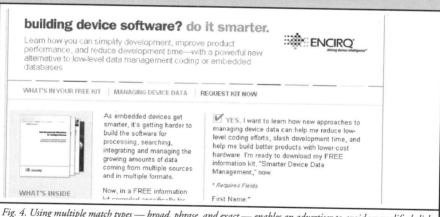

Fig. 4. Using multiple match types — broad, phrase, and exact — enables an advertiser to avoid unqualified clicks and determine precisely which terms and phrases are performing most efficiently.

Mistake #5: Too Few Keywords

Most search marketers set up their Google program with only a very basic, relatively short list of keywords. To do more, here again, is an investment of time and resources that most companies figures they can do without. Plus, most advertisers mistakenly equate a longer list of keywords with higher expense when in fact too few keywords can have a very detrimental effect on program efficiency.

Why Your Google Campaign Isn't Working and What to Do About It

When we inherit search programs from clients, we typically increase the number of keywords by anywhere from five to ten times or more. A small segment of that increase will be additional, unique terms that the client neglected to include (see: Mistake #6, page 10), but the vast majority will be variations on existing terms: plurals, misspellings, phrases, etc.

For example, a company marketing "anti-virus software" should also include "anti virus software" (without the hyphen), "enterprise anti-virus software," "antivirus software free trial," and so on — basically, every relevant variation possible that includes the key root words.

It's not difficult to see why most clients don't bother with the time and effort required to expand their keyword list. After all, in the example above, a broad match on "anti virus software" would capture many of the same searches. The reason to expand the list nonetheless is two-fold: First, there will always be some subset of prospects that use a minor variation of your existing keywords (a plural term, perhaps, or a common misspelling), that you otherwise wouldn't reach. Second, selecting keywords intelligently is not a matter of capturing all possible searches with the shortest list of terms (translation: the minimum amount of effort and complexity).

Contrary to intuition, a shorter list of keywords (probably employing broad match types) is more expensive, because it's likely to generate a high percentage of unqualified clicks. Conversely, a more expansive list of terms will be more efficient because it enables you to zero in on those precise terms and phrases that generate the lowest CPA.

One of the easiest and most effective ways to expand your keyword list is through the use of negative keywords. Negative keywords are one of the most overlooked and under utilized tools for significantly reducing wasteful spending on irrelevant and unqualified clicks. Negative keywords work like filters which prevent ads from showing when queries include keywords that you deem to be irrelevant.

Negative keywords can be applied at both the campaign and ad group level. At the campaign level, an advertiser can apply the most obvious negative terms, those terms that are irrelevant in any situation in which your ads could possibly be triggered. For example, a company marketing high-priced, enterprise software would be wise to include "free" as a campaign negative. Doing so will prevent ads displaying on searches by individuals looking for freeware.

At the ad group level, negative keywords can be used to ensure visitors are guided to the preferred landing page or microsite. For example, a seller of new and used office equipment might use "new" as a negative in the used furniture ad group, and "used" in the new furniture ad group.

Why Your Google Campaign Isn't Working and What to Do About It

There are always keywords that can be added to your program. Furthermore, there is no penalty for doing so. A well-managed Google program evolves and attains ever greater levels of performance as new keywords are constantly tested and introduced to the program.

Mistake #6: Thinking Like a Marketer and Not Like Your Audience

Many advertisers make the mistake of regarding their search program as a means to find only that exclusive group of highly qualified prospects who are actively searching for their type of product. This results in a program with a relatively short list of keywords, all of which are highly product-related.

Google and other search programs can be an effective way to engage with prospects actively researching a specific type of product. However, the vast majority of prospects, particularly if your company isn't well known or if you compete in a nascent product category, will not be searching for your product or service. They're looking for a solution to their problem. For example, a prospect in need of a CRM solution may not be searching on "CRM software." He or she may be searching on "improve customer service."

Smart search marketers put themselves in the position of their potential customer. Are there other terms related to the symptoms of the problem that differ from terms specific to the solution? Are users, influencers, and evangelists likely to be searching on different terms compared to decision-makers? Are there differences between geographical regions or target markets?

Test any and all keywords that might be applicable to your product or the problem that your product solves. Include branded terms and industry jargon. Scan industry Web sites to pick up phrases and words you might not have considered otherwise. Most prospects will use terms that make complete sense to them, but are not used by your firm in a marketing context. Test as many keywords as possible, and then let the market — your potential customers — decide how they want to describe the solution they're looking for.

Mistake #7: Selling the Product, Not the Offer

Google allows a total of 105 characters in their text ads, including spaces. It's therefore pointless to waste this precious space on fluff. Here again, many search marketers make the mistake of describing their company or product in their ad, on the erroneous assumption that keyword advertising is fundamentally about promoting a product.

The only instance where brand messaging — promoting your company or product explicitly — generally works is with branded terms (for instance, the name of your

Why Your Google Campaign Isn't Working and What to Do About It

company or product), and even then, most companies don't have a strong enough brand to pull it off. Using the ad copy to sing the praises of your company is usually a recipe for disastrous results, particularly in combination with search terms more related to the relevant problem (see previous page) than your product.

Network Performance	Boost Network Performance
83 Fortune 100 companies rely on	Free Information Kit explains how
Acme Global Services	White papers, case studies, more.
www.acme.net	www.acme.net

Fig. 5. Brand-oriented copy in search ads is rarely effective except on branded terms. More direct, response-oriented copy that includes a clear offer and compelling benefits is typically more successful.

Think of your ad not as a billboard for your product, but rather as a tool to capture and engage with prospects suffering from the issue, problem, or challenge that your product or service can solve. Try to sell your company too soon, and you'll turn people off. Conversely, more informational, offer-oriented ads will engage prospects more readily.

In general, effective ad copy should:

- Contain a specific and tangible offer (a free trial, an information kit)

- State clearly why the searcher needs to take action ("find out how ...", "learn 10 secrets ...")

- Qualify the visitor by extolling benefits that will interest the right type of prospect

Effective, response-oriented ad copy is direct and to the point, and above all, relevant to the search term. Some of the most successful search ads don't mention the advertiser's name at all, except in the display URL. Instead, they include the precise search term or phrase (see the discussion of campaign infrastructure and multiple ad groups on page 7), present a compelling offer, and state a clear benefit as to why the prospect needs to act.

Remember: Google allows search marketers to run multiple ads against batches of keywords or even single keywords. Your search program is a highly efficient platform for testing offers, calls to action, landing pages, etc., all of which can leads to higher efficiency and better results.

Mistake #8: Uninformed Use of Google's Content Network

Google allows for three ways to have your search ads distributed: 1) Google proper

Why Your Google Campaign Isn't Working and What to Do About It

(ie: the site itself); 2) Google's search network; and 3) Google's content network. The key distinction between Google's search network and the content network is that in the latter, the impressions are not search-based. When you advertise on the content network, your ad is served when an individual views content that Google deems to be relevant to your selected keywords. This is very different user behavior compared to someone searching on a term, either on Google itself or one of their partner search sites.

Including the content network as part of your Google search program is a default setting when you set up your account. Continued use of the content network without analyzing the results separate from the rest of the program is one of the most common — and most expensive — mistakes that search marketers make.

Because of the scope of the content network and the nature of how impressions are served, it's highly likely that, left to run unchecked, the content network will:

1) Generate far more impressions than the search network

2) Generate a much lower click-through rate (CTR)

3) Burn through a large proportion of your overall spend

4) Decrease overall program efficiency

Ad Network	Status	Current Bid Max CPC	Clicks	Impr.	CTR	Avg. CPC	Cost	Avg. Pos
Google + search network (?)	Enabled	Default $2.00 Edit	24	7,111	0.33%	$2.12	$50.93	2.8
Content network (?)	Disabled		329	985,362	0.03%	$1.29	$425.08	2.7
Total			353	992,473	0.33%	$2.12	$476.01	2.8

Fig. 6. Unfettered use of Google's content network can often result in a large proportion of monthly spend dedicated to clicks that convert to leads at a much lower rate.

Like the search network, the content network is performance-based; you will only incur cost when clicks occur. However, our experience is that these clicks tend to be far less targeted than search-based clicks. While Google does offer the ability to set bid rates lower for content clicks, and also exclude specific sites from the content network, inexperienced search marketers tend to not use either option. As a result, without sufficient time and resources expended on monitoring the value of traffic from the content network, the result is usually a much higher Cost Per Acquisition (CPA).

We're not contending that the content network has no merit. However, if you're not tracking and analyzing results from the content network separately, you won't know if it has merit or not. In the majority of cases, if left to run unmanaged, it hurts more than it helps. When starting a search program on Google, we typically recommend selecting

Why Your Google Campaign Isn't Working and What to Do About It

"Google search" only in the "Networks" option under Campaign Settings (see: Mistake #9, below). As the program stabilizes and more exposure is warranted, and once you have a better idea which terms and phrases are generating the lowest CPA, consider adding the search and content networks — in that order.

Note: There is much industry discussion of late on the topic of click fraud. Our experience has been that fraud is much more prevalent when the content network is used. To Google's credit, they have rolled out features to better enable improvement in the quality of the content-based impressions, but using these features requires time and knowledge.

Mistake #9: Not Leveraging Campaign Level Settings

At the campaign level, search marketers have a number of useful features available to them in Google, all of which can improve the efficiency of a search program. However, most search marketers fail to take advantage of these features, and, in addition, make the mistake of consolidating their entire program into one campaign.

Note: These features are exponentially more valuable when they're used to calibrate multiple campaigns within one program, rather than as global settings for one master campaign. We always set up multiple campaigns for each client, each campaign tailored to a specific objective. (Tip: When you set up multiple campaigns, don't use "Campaign 1," "Campaign 2," etc. More descriptive names will facilitate management.)

Here's a review of some of the most useful features available at the campaign level:

- Run Date: If there are time-sensitive elements to campaigns (for example, a trade show, price promotion, or product launch), use the run date settings to automatically end the campaign at a certain date. This helps avoid disgruntled searchers who might click on an ad looking for a specific offer only to find it no longer valid on the site.

- Keyword Bidding: We recommend not using the Google Budget Optimizer and to stick with manual bidding. The intent of the Budget Optimizer is to maximize clicks within a given budget; however, our point of view is that clicks only represent a cost to the advertiser (or put another way, revenue to Google). If your goal is to turn as many clicks as possible into leads or customers and do so at the lowest possible CPA, keyword bidding will give you greater precision.

- Ad Scheduling: This is an overlooked feature that can be particularly effective for B2B advertisers. Because most prospects for business solutions will conduct searches while at work, an advertiser can concentrate his or her media spend over the hours when the target audience is most likely to be at work. This can be an effective way to "stretch" a media budget by eliminating impressions — and

Why Your Google Campaign Isn't Working and What to Do About It

unqualified clicks — during the time of when qualified prospects are much less likely to be conducting searches. Keep in mind that the ad scheduling timetable in Google is based on the time zone you specified when you set up your account. So, if you're in Los Angeles, you'll want to ensure that you have your ads active at the appropriate time on the East Coast. Google also offers an Advanced Ad Scheduling feature so you can raise or lower your bids at specific times of the day if you've identified those times as more critical.

- Countries and Territories: If your target can be segmented geographically, consider doing so. For example, if your company can realistically only support (or effectively sell to) U.S. or North American customers, select only the appropriate geography. Or if Europe is also a key marketplace, establish separate European-focused campaigns using your North American campaigns as a template. Then leverage settings for the non-North American campaign and optimize accordingly. Don't, under any circumstances, mix campaigns across continents.

Using campaign settings like those described here will result in higher-quality traffic but can also result in fewer impressions and even fewer clicks overall. Remember, an effective search program is not just about volume; it's about efficiency. Campaign settings are a useful way to zero in on the good, and concentrate your spending where it's most likely to generate qualified prospects. Keep in mind, however, that efficiency is only really measured through some kind of conversion tracking. Otherwise, you'll have a much tougher time explaining to your boss why lowering click volume is a good thing.

Mistake #10: Ego Bidding

By "ego bidding" we mean the strategy of securing the top position (or one of the top positions) for a particular search term, regardless of cost or efficiency. Ego bidding is frequently a strategy dictated by vice presidents or other top executives. They want to see the company's name in lights, or at the very least above their closest competitor.

The only guarantee that comes with targeting the number one position is a big bill from Google at the end of the month. At the number one position, conversions (the ratio of clicks to leads) are generally lower and acquisition cost more expensive. Why? First, because you'll need to outbid your competitors to achieve that top position, and second, because many search users click on the top ad instinctually, without regard to relevance. The result is a large number of expensive, unqualified clicks that don't turn into real prospects.

It's rarely advisable to have a strategy of securing the top position for a particular term unless 1) it's part of a short-term strategy to maximize visibility (for example, as part of a product launch), or 2.) if past data indicates it's a profitable position —

Why Your Google Campaign Isn't Working and What to Do About It

that is, where the higher bid cost has been offset by a higher conversion rate and thus a lower CPA.

About Point It!

Point It! is a full service search engine marketing agency specializing in lead acquisition programs for technology and B2B companies. The company serves a broad range of clients, ranging from startups to tech industry giants, from its offices in the shadow of the Space Needle in Seattle, Washington.

About the Author

Eric Layland is Vice President of Client Operations and co-founder of Point It!. Prior to Point It!, he served as a marketing consultant to technology and ecommerce firms from start-up through initial public offering or acquisition. In 1996 Eric joined one of the first online lead generation agencies. During his tenure he directed teams chartered with management of strategic relationships, corporate development and launched his first paid search program on GoTo.com (now Yahoo! Search) in 1997.

Point It! Inc.
2200 Sixth Avenue
Suite 260
Seattle, WA 98121
206-525-3000
206-374-1300
www.pointit.com
info@pointit.com

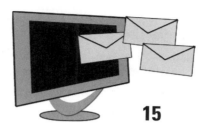

15

RECOMMENDED GOOGLE & SEO LIBRARY

I recommend you build a quality reference library to assist you with your overall e-commerce online marketing portfolio and SEO. While there are plenty of excellent books on the market, I definitely recommend you add the following to your library. All are available through Atlantic Publishing Company (**www.atlantic-pub.com**), as well as Amazon (**www.amazon. com**), and Barnes & Noble (**www.bn.com**):

How to Use the Internet to Advertise, Promote and Market Your Business or Web Site—With Little or No Money

Interested in promoting your business and/ or Web site, but don't have the big budget for traditional advertising? This new book will show you how to build, promote, and make money off your Web site or brick and mortar store using the Internet, with minimal costs. Let us arm you with the knowledge you need to make your business a success! Learn how to generate more traffic for your site or store with hundreds of Internet marketing methods, including many free and low-cost promotions.

This new book presents a comprehensive, hands-on, step-by-step guide for increasing Web site traffic and traditional store traffic by using hundreds of proven tips, tools, and techniques. Learn how to target more customers to your business and optimize your Web site from a marketing perspective. You will learn to target your campaign, use keywords, generate free advertising, search-engine strategies, learn the inside secrets of e-mail marketing, how to build Web communities, co-branding, auto-responders, Google advertising, banner advertising, eBay storefronts, Web-design information, search-engine registration, directories, and real-world examples of what strategies are succeeding and what strategies are failing.

Online Marketing Success Stories: Insider Secrets from the Experts Who Are Making Millions on the Internet Today

Standing out in the turmoil of today's Internet marketplace is a major challenge. There are many books and courses on Internet marketing; this is the only book that will provide you with insider secrets. We asked the marketing experts who make their living on the Internet every day — and they talked. Online Marketing Success Stories will give you real-life examples of how successful busine businesses market their products online. The information is so useful that you can read a page and put the idea into action — today!

With e-commerce expected to reach $40 billion and online businesses anticipated to increase by 500 percent through 2010, your business needs guidance from today's successful Internet marketing veterans. Learn the most efficient ways to bring consumers to your site, get visitors to purchase, how to up-sell, oversights to avoid, and

how to steer clear of years of disappointment.

We spent thousands of hours interviewing, e-mailing, and communicating with hundreds of today's most successful e-commerce marketers. This book not only chronicles their achievements, but is a compilation of their secrets and proven successful ideas. If you are interested in learning hundreds of hints, tricks, and secrets on how to make money (or more money) with your Web site, then this book is for you.

Instruction is great, but advice from experts is even better, and the experts chronicled in this book are earning millions. This new exhaustively researched book will provide you with a jam-packed assortment of innovative ideas that you can put to use today. This book gives you the proven strategies, innovative ideas, and actual case studies to help you sell more with less time and effort.

The Ultimate Guide to Search Engine Marketing: Pay Per Click Advertising Secrets Revealed

Is your ultimate goal to have more customers come to your Web site? You can increase your Web site traffic by more than 1,000 percent through the expert execution of pay per click advertising. With PPC advertising you are only drawing highly qualified visitors to your Web site. PPC brings you fast results and you can reach your target audience with the most cost effective method on the Internet today.

Pay per click, or PPC, is an advertising technique that uses search engines where you can display your text ads throughout the Internet keyed to the type of business you have or the type of products you are promoting. Successful PPC advertising ensures that your text ads reach the right audience while your business only pays for the clicks your ads receive!

Master the art and science behind pay per click advertising in a matter of hours. By investing a few dollars you can easily increase the number of visitors to your Web site and significantly increase sales! If you are looking to drive high quality, targeted traffic to your site, there is no better way than to use cost per click advertising. Since you only pay when someone actually clicks on your ad, your marketing dollars are being used more effectively and efficiently compared to any other advertising method.

By 2010, online marketers will spend $7 billion dollars on PPC advertising (JupiterResearch). Thousands of companies will waste precious advertising dollars this year on ineffective or poorly organized PPC campaigns. There is an art form to this method of advertising, and that is what this new book is all about. In this book we show you the secrets of executing a successful, cost-effective campaign.

The key to success in PPC advertising is to know what you are doing, devise a comprehensive and well-crafted advertising plan, and know the relationships between your Web site, search engines, and PPC advertising campaign methodology. This groundbreaking and exhaustively researched new book will provide everything you need to know to get you started on generating high-volume, high quality leads to your Web site. This new book will teach you the six steps to a successful campaign: Keyword Research, Copy Editing, Setup and Implementation, Bid Management, Performance Analysis, Return on Investment, and Reporting and Avoiding PPC Fraud.

In addition, we spent thousands of hours interviewing hundreds of today's most successful PPC masters. This book is a compilation of their secrets and proven successful ideas. Additionally, we give you hundreds of tips and tricks to ensure your Web site is optimized for maximum search engine effectiveness to drive business to your Web site and increase sales and profits. In this book you will find actual case studies from companies who have used our techniques and achieved unprecedented success. If you are interested in learning hundreds of hints, tricks, and secrets on how to implement pay per click advertising, optimize your Web site for maximum search engine effectiveness, develop a cost-effective marketing campaign, and ultimately earn enormous profits, then this book is for you.

The Complete Guide to E-mail Marketing: How to Create Successful, Spam-Free Campaigns to Reach Your Target Audience and Increase Sales

Researchers estimate that by 2008 e-mail marketing revenues will surpass $1.8 billion dollars annually. Are you getting your share? According to Jupiter Research, 93 percent of U.S. Internet users consider e-mail their top online activity. E-mail is a fast, inexpensive, and highly effective way to target and address your audience. Companies like Microsoft, Amazon. com, Yahoo, as well as most Fortune 1000 firms, are using responsible e-mail marketing for one simple reason. It works! And it generates profits immediately and consistently!

In this new groundbreaking book you will learn how to create top-notch e-mail marketing campaigns, how to build stronger customer relationships, generate new qualified leads and sales, learn insider secrets to build your e-mail list quickly, deal with spam filters, and the optimum days and times to send your e-mails.

You will have step-by-step ways to:

- Build your business quickly using responsible, ethical e-mail marketing

- Leverage your current Web site, using auto responders

- Write effective e-mail advertising copy

- Develop newsletters

- Write winning subject lines

- Get high click-through rates

- Format your messages

- Put the subscription form on your site

- Use pop ups

- Use single or double opt-in subscriptions

- Increase the response rate of your offer dramatically

- Format your e-mail so that it will be received and read

- Choose between text or HTML e-mail (and why)

- Reduce advertising expenses

- Have measurable marketing results with instant feedback

- Automate the whole e-mail marketing process

In addition, we spent thousands of hours interviewing, e-mailing, and communicating with hundreds of today's most successful e-mail marketing experts. This book contains their secrets and proven successful ideas, including actual case studies. If you are interested in learning hundreds of hints, strategies, and secrets on how to implement effective e-mail marketing campaigns and ultimately earn enormous profits, then this book is for you.

AUTHOR DEDICATION & BIOGRAPHY

This book is dedicated to The Tedster.

Bruce C. Brown is the best-selling author of *How to Use the Internet to Advertise, Promote, and Market Your Business or Web Site With Little or No Money* and recently published his third book, *The Ultimate Guide to Search Engine Marketing: Pay-Per-Click Advertising Secrets Revealed*. Bruce is finishing his 23rd year as an officer in the United States Coast Guard and is looking forward to retirement when he can concentrate on helping others succeed with their online businesses and marketing campaigns. He uses his 20-plus years of expertise in financial management in conjunction with more than 12 years as a Web designer, business owner, e-marketing consultant, and hardware and software specialist. He completed college during his military career, earning degrees from the University of Phoenix and Charter Oak State College. He currently splits his time between Washington, DC, and Land O Lakes, Florida, with his wife Vonda and youngest son, Colton. His oldest son, Dalton, is a full-time student at the University of South Florida in Tampa (Go Bulls!), and his middle son, Jordan, is a full-time student at the University of Florida in Gainesville (Go Gators!).

GLOSSARY

LINKING STRATEGY

Link checker: Tool used to check for broken hyperlinks.

Deep linking: Linking to a Web page other than a site's home page.

Inbound link: A link from a site outside of your site.

Outbound link: A link to a site outside of your site.

Reciprocal links: Links between two sites, often based on an agreement by the site owners to exchange links.

INTERNET ADVERTISING DEFINITIONS AND TERMS

The following definitions about Internet advertising terms and definitions will give you a better understanding of some of the many Web advertising concepts you need to learn so that you can successfully advertise on the Internet.

Source for terms and definitions: **http://searchcio.techtarget.com/sDefinition/0,,sid19_gci211535,00.html**

Ad Impression: An ad impression, or ad view, occurs when a user pulls up a Web page through a browser and sees an ad that is served on that page. Many Web sites sell advertising space by ad impressions.

Ad rotation: Ads are often rotated into ad spaces from a list. This is usually done automatically by software on the Web site or at a central site administered by an ad broker or server facility for a network of Web sites.

Ad space: An ad space is a space on a Web page that is reserved for ads. An ad space group is a group of spaces within a Web site that share the same characteristics so that an ad purchase can be made for the group of spaces.

Ad view: An ad view, synonymous with ad impression, is a single ad that appears on a Web page when the page arrives at the viewer's display. Ad views are what most Web sites sell or prefer to sell. A Web page may offer space for a number of ad views. In general, the term impression is more commonly used.

Ad: For Web advertising, an ad is almost always a banner, a graphic image, or set of animated images (in a file called an animated GIF) of a designated pixel size and byte size limit. An ad or set of ads for a campaign is often referred to as "the creative." Banners and other special advertising that include an interactive or visual element beyond the usual are known as rich media.

Advertising network: A network representing many Web sites in selling advertising, allowing advertising buyers to reach broad audiences relatively easily through run-of-category and run-of-network buys.

Affiliate: The publisher/salesperson in an affiliate marketing relationship.

Affiliate Marketing: Revenue sharing between online advertisers/

merchants and online publishers/salespeople, whereby compensation is based on performance measures, typically in the form of sales, clicks, registrations, or a hybrid model. Affiliate marketing is the use by a Web site that sells products of other Web sites, called affiliates, to help market the products. Amazon created the first large-scale affiliate program and hundreds of other companies have followed since.

Affiliate Merchant: The advertiser in an affiliate marketing relationship.

Affiliate Network: A value-added intermediary providing services, including aggregation, for affiliate merchants and affiliates.

Affiliate Software: Software that, at a minimum, provides tracking and reporting of commission-triggering actions (sales, registrations, or clicks) from affiliate links.

Banner: A banner is an advertisement in the form of a graphic image that typically runs across a Web page or is positioned in a margin or other space reserved for ads. Banner ads are usually Graphics Interchange Format (GIF) images. In addition to adhering to size, many Web sites limit the size of the file to a certain number of bytes so that the file will display quickly. Most ads are animated GIFs since animation has been shown to attract a larger percentage of user clicks. The most common larger banner ad is 468 pixels wide by 60 pixels high. Smaller sizes include 125 by 125 and 120 by 90 pixels. These and other banner sizes have been established as standard sizes by the Internet Advertising Bureau.

Beyond the banner: This is the idea that, in addition to banner ads, there are other ways to use the Internet to communicate a marketing message. These include sponsoring a Web site or a particular feature on it; advertising in e-mail newsletters; co-branding with another company and its Web site; contest promotion; and, in general, finding new ways to engage and interact with the desired audience. "Beyond the banner" approaches can also include the interstitial and streaming video infomercial. The banner itself can be transformed into a small rich media event.

Booked space: This is the number of ad views for an ad space that are currently sold out.

Brand, brand name, and branding: A brand is a product, service, or concept that is publicly distinguished from other products, services, or concepts so that it can be easily communicated and usually marketed. A brand name is the name of the distinctive product, service, or concept. Branding is the process of creating and disseminating the brand name. Branding can be applied to the entire corporate identity as well as to individual product and service names. In Web and other media advertising, it is recognized that there is usually some kind of branding value whether or not an immediate, direct response can be measured from an ad or campaign. Companies like Proctor and Gamble have made a science out of creating and evaluating the success of their brand name products.

Caching: The storage of Web files for later re-use at a point more quickly accessed by the end user.

Cache server: In Internet advertising, the caching of pages in a cache server or the user's computer means that some ad views won't be known by the ad counting programs and is a source of concern. There are several techniques for telling the browser not to cache particular pages. On the other hand, specifying no caching for all pages may mean that users will find your site to be slower than you would like.

Campaign: A campaign consists of one or more ad groups. The ads in a given campaign share the same daily budget, language and location targeting, end dates, and distribution options.

Click rate: The click rate is the percentage of ad views that resulted in click-throughs. Although there is visibility and branding value in ad views that don't result in a click-through, this value is difficult to measure. A click-through has several values: it's an indication of the ad's effectiveness, and it results in the viewer getting to the advertiser's Web site where other messages can be provided. A new approach is for a click to result not in a link to another site but to an immediate product order window. What a successful click rate is depends on a number of factors, such as the campaign objectives, how enticing the banner message is, how explicit the message is (a message that is complete within the banner may be less apt to be clicked), audience/message matching, how new the banner is, how often it is displayed to the same user, and so forth. In general, click rates for high-repeat, branding banners vary from 0.15 to 1 percent. Ads with provocative, mysterious, or other compelling content can induce click rates ranging from 1 to 5 percent and sometimes higher. The click rate for a given ad tends to diminish with repeated exposure.

Click stream: A click stream is a recorded path of the pages a user requested in going through one or more Web sites. Click stream information can help Web site owners understand how visitors are using their site and which pages are getting the most use. It can help advertisers understand how users get to the client's pages, what pages they look at, and how they go about ordering a product.

Click: According to ad industry recommended guidelines from FAST, a click is "when a visitor interacts with an advertisement." This does not apparently mean simply interacting with a rich media ad, but actually clicking on it so that the visitor is headed toward the advertiser's destination. It also does not mean that the visitor actually waits to fully arrive at the destination, but just that the visitor started going there.

Click-through: A click-through is what is counted by the sponsoring site as a result of an ad click. In practice, click and click-through tend to be used interchangeably. A click-through, however, seems to imply that the user actually received the page. A few advertisers are willing to pay only for click-throughs rather than for ad impressions.

Click-through Rate: The cost of one click-through for a banner ad.

Co-branding: Co-branding on the Web often means two Web sites or Web site sections or features displaying their logos (and thus their brands) together so that the viewer considers the site or feature to be a joint enterprise. Co-branding is often associated with cross-linking between the sites, although it isn't necessary.

Conversion Rate: The percentage of site visitors who respond to the desired goal of an ad campaign compared with the total number of people who see the ad campaign. The goal may be, for example, convincing readers to become subscribers, encouraging customers to buy something, or enticing prospective customers from another site with an ad.

Cookie: A cookie is a file on a Web user's hard drive (it's kept in one of the subdirectories under the browser file directory) that is used by Web sites to record data about the user. Some ad rotation software uses cookies to see which ad the user has just seen so that a different ad will be rotated into the next page view.

Cost-per-action: Cost-per-action is what an advertiser pays for each visitor that takes some specifically defined action in response to an ad beyond simply clicking on it. For example, a visitor might visit an advertiser's site and request to be subscribe to its newsletter.

Cost-per-click (CPC): The amount of money an advertiser will pay to a site each time a user clicks on an ad or link.

Cost-per-lead: This is a more specific form of cost-per-action in which a visitor provides enough information at the advertiser's site, or in interaction with a rich media ad, to be used as a sales lead. Note that you can estimate cost-per-lead regardless of how you pay for the ad. In other words, buying on a pay-per-lead basis is not required to calculate the cost-per-lead.

Cost-per-sale: Sites that sell products directly from their Web site or can otherwise determine sales generated as the result of an advertising sales lead can calculate the cost-per-sale of Web advertising.

CPA: See cost-per-action.

CPC: See cost-per-click.

CPM: CPM is "cost per thousand" ad impressions, an industry standard measure for selling ads on Web sites. This measure is taken from print advertising. The "M" has nothing to do with "mega" or million. It's taken from the Roman numeral for "thousand."

CPS: See cost-per-sale.

CPTM: CPTM is "cost per thousand targeted" ad impressions, apparently implying that the audience you're selling is targeted to particular demographics.

Creative: Ad agencies and buyers often refer to ad banners and other forms of created advertising as "the creative." Since the creative requires creative inspiration and skill that may come from a third party, it often does not arrive until late in the preparation for a new campaign launch.

CTR: See click-through rate.

Demographics: Demographics is data about the size and characteristics of a population or audience, for example, gender, age group, income group, purchasing history, personal preferences, and so forth.

Domains: Registered domain name (with name server record).

FAST: FAST is a coalition of the Internet Advertising Bureau, the ANA, and the ARF that has recommended or is working on guidelines for consumer privacy, ad models and creative formats, audience and ad impression measurement, and a standard reporting template together with a standard insertion order. FAST originated with Proctor and Gamble's Future of Advertising Stakeholders Summit in August 1998. FAST's first guideline, available in March 1999, was a guideline on "Basic Advertising Measures." Our definitions in this list include the FAST definitions for impression and click.

Filtering: Filtering is the immediate analysis by a program of a user Web page request in order to determine which ad or ads to return in the requested page. A Web page request can tell a Web site or its ad server whether it fits a certain characteristic such as coming from a particular company's address or that the user is using a particular level of browser. The Web ad server can respond accordingly.

Fold: "Above the fold," a term borrowed from print media, refers to an ad that is viewable as soon as the Web page arrives. You don't have to scroll down (or sideways) to see it. Since screen resolution can affect what is immediately viewable, it's good to know whether the Web site's audience tends to set their resolution at 640 by 480 pixels or at 800 by 600 (or higher).

Frequency cap: Restriction on the amount of times a specific visitor is shown a particular advertisement.

Hit: A hit is the sending of a single file whether an HTML file, an image, an audio file, or other file type. Since a single Web page request can bring with it a number of individual files, the number of hits from a site is a not a good indication of its actual use (number of visitors). It does have meaning for the Web site space provider, however, as an indicator of traffic flow.

House ad: Self-promotional ad a company runs on its media outlets to put unsold inventory to use.

Impression: According to the "Basic Advertising Measures," from FAST, an ad industry group, an impression is "The count of a delivered basic advertising unit from an ad distribution point." Impressions are how most Web advertising is sold and the cost is quoted in terms of the cost per thousand impressions (CPM).

Insertion order: An insertion order is a formal, printed order to run an ad campaign. Typically, the insertion order identifies the campaign name, the Web site receiving the order and the planner or buyer giving the order, the individual ads to be run (or who will provide them), the ad sizes, the campaign beginning and end dates, the CPM, the total cost, discounts to be applied, and reporting requirements and possible penalties or stipulations relative to the failure to deliver the impressions.

Internet: The millions of computers that are linked together around the world, allowing any computer to communicate with any other that is part of the network

Inventory: Inventory is the total number of ad views or impressions that a Web site has to sell over a given period of time (usually, inventory is figured by the month).

IO: See insertion order.

Keyword marketing: Putting your message in front of people who are searching using particular keywords and key phrases.

Keyword Matching Options: There are four types of keyword matching: broad matching, exact matching, phrase matching, and negative keywords. These options help you refine your ad targeting on Google search pages.

Keyword Searches: Searches for specific words.

Maximum Cost-per-click (CPC): With keyword-targeted ad campaigns, you choose the maximum cost-per-click (max CPC) you are willing to pay.

Maximum Cost-per-impression (CPM): With site-targeted ad campaigns, you choose the maximum cost per thousand impressions (Max CPM) you are willing to pay.

Meta Tags: Hidden HTML directions for Web browsers or search engines. They include important information, such as the title of each page, relevant keywords describing site content, and the description of the site that shows up when a search engine returns a search.

Media broker: Since it's often not efficient for an advertiser to select every Web site it wants to put ads on, media brokers aggregate sites for advertisers and their media planners and buyers, based on demographics and other factors.

Media buyer: A media buyer, usually at an advertising agency, works with a media planner to allocate the money provided for an advertising campaign among specific print or online media (magazines, TV, Web sites, and so forth), and then calls and places the advertising orders. On the Web, placing the order often includes requesting proposals and negotiating the final cost.

Networks: Registered class A/B/C addresses.

Opt-in e-mail: Opt-in e-mail is e-mail containing information or advertising that users explicitly request (opt) to receive. Typically, a Web site invites its visitors to fill out forms identifying subject or product categories that interest them and about which they are willing to receive e-mail from anyone who might send it. The Web site sells the names (with explicit or implicit permission from their visitors) to a company that specializes in collecting mailing lists that represent different interests. Whenever the mailing list company sells its lists to advertisers, the Web site is paid a small amount for each name that it generated for the list. You can sometimes identify opt-in e-mail because it starts with a statement that tells you that you have previously agreed to receive such messages.

Page Impressions: A measure of how many times a Web page has been displayed to visitors. Often used as a crude way of counting the visitors to a site.

Page Requests: A measure of the number of pages that visitors have viewed in a day. Often used as a crude way of indicating the popularity of your Web site.

Paid Search: The area of keyword, contextual advertising, often called pay-per-click

Page View: A common metric for measuring how many times a complete page is visited.

Pay-per-click: In pay-per-click advertising, the advertiser pays a certain amount for each click-through to the advertiser's Web site. The amount paid per click-through is arranged at the time of the insertion order and varies considerably. Higher pay-per-click rates recognize that there may be some "no-click" branding value as well as click-through value provided.

Pay-per-lead: In pay-per-lead advertising, the advertiser pays for each sales lead generated. For example, an advertiser might pay for every visitor that clicked on a site and then filled out a form.

Pay-per-sale: Pay-per-sale is not customarily used for ad buys. It is, however, the customary way to pay Web sites that participate in affiliate programs, such as those of Amazon.com and Beyond.com.

Pay-per-view: Since this is the prevalent type of ad buying arrangement at larger Web sites, this term tends to be used only when comparing this most prevalent method with pay-per-click and other methods.

Proof of performance: Some advertisers may want proof that the ads they've bought have actually run and that click-through figures are accurate. In print media, tear sheets taken from a publication prove that an ad was run. On the Web, there is no industry-wide practice for proof of performance. Some buyers rely on the integrity of the media broker and the Web site. The ad buyer usually checks the Web site to determine the ads are actually running. Most buyers require weekly figures during a campaign. A few want to look directly at the figures, viewing the ad server or Web site reporting tool.

Psychographic characteristics: This is a term for personal interest information that is gathered by Web sites by requesting it from users. For example, a Web site could ask users to list the Web sites that they visit most often. Advertisers could use this data to help create a demographic profile for that site.

Rate card: Document detailing prices for various ad placement options.

Rep firm: Ad sales partner specializing primarily in single-site sales.

Reporting template: Although the media have to report data to ad agencies and media planners and buyers during and at the end of each campaign, no standard report is yet available. FAST, the ad industry coalition, is working on a proposed standard reporting template that would enable reporting to be consistent.

Rich media: Rich media is advertising that contains perceptual or interactive elements more elaborate than the usual banner ad. Today, the term is often used for banner ads with popup menus that let the visitor select a particular page to link to on the advertiser's site. Rich media ads are generally more challenging to create and to serve. Some early studies have shown that rich media ads tend to be more effective than ordinary animated banner ads.

ROI: ROI (return on investment) is "the bottom line" on how successful an ad or campaign was in terms of what the returns, generally sales revenue, were for the money expended (invested).

RON: See run-of-network.

ROS: See run-of-site.

Run-of-network: A run-of-network ad is one that is placed to run on all sites within a given network of sites. Ad sales firms handle run-of-network insertion orders in such a way as to optimize results for the buyer consistent with higher priority ad commitments.

Run-of-site: A run-of-site ad is one that is placed to rotate on all nonfeatured ad spaces on a site. CPM rates for run-of-site ads are usually less than for rates for specially-placed ads or sponsorships.

Search Engine Marketing (SEM): Promoting a Web site through a search engine. This most often refers to targeting prospective customers by buying relevant keywords or phrases.

Search Engine: A special site that provides an index of other Web site addresses listed according to key words and descriptions in the original page.

Search Engine Optimization (SEO): Making a Web site more friendly to search engines, resulting in a higher page rank.

Self-serve advertising: Advertising that can be purchased without the assistance of a sales representative.

Splash page: A splash page (also known as an interstitial) is a preliminary page that precedes the regular home page of a Web site and usually promotes a particular site feature or provides advertising. A splash page is timed to move on to the home page after a short period of time.

Sponsor: Depending on the context, a sponsor simply means an advertiser who has sponsored an ad and, by doing so, has also helped sponsor or sustain the Web site itself. It can also mean an advertiser that has a special relationship with the Web site and supports a special feature of a Web site, such as a writer's column, a Flower-of-the-Day, or a collection of articles on a particular subject.

Sponsorship: Sponsorship is an association with a Web site in some way that gives an advertiser some particular visibility and advantage above that of run-of-site advertising. When associated with specific content, sponsorship can provide a more targeted audience than run-of-site ad buys. Sponsorship also implies a "synergy and resonance" between the Web site and the advertiser. Some sponsorships are available as value-added opportunities for advertisers who buy a certain minimum amount of advertising.

Targeting: Targeting is purchasing ad space on Web sites that match audience and campaign objective requirements. Techtarget.com, with over 20 Web sites targeted to special information technology audiences, is an example of an online publishing business built to enable advertising targeting.

Underdelivery: Delivery of fewer impressions, visitors, or conversions than contracted for a specified period of time.

Unique visitor: A unique visitor is someone with a unique address who is entering a Web site for the first time that day (or some other specified period). Thus, a visitor that returns within the same day is not counted twice. A unique visitors count tells you how many different people there are in your audience during the time period, but not how much they used the site during the period.

User session: A user session is someone with a unique address that enters or reenters a Web site each day (or some other specified period). A user session is sometimes determined by counting only those users that haven't reentered the site within the past 20 minutes or a similar period. User session figures are sometimes used, somewhat incorrectly, to indicate "visits" or "visitors" per day. User sessions are a better indicator of total site activity than "unique visitors" since they indicate frequency of use.

View: A view is, depending on what's meant, either an ad view or a page view. Usually an ad view is what's meant. There can be multiple ad views per page views. View counting should consider that a small percentage of users choose to turn the graphics off (not display the images) in their browser.

Visit: A visit is a Web user with a unique address entering a Web site at some page for the first time that day (or for the first time in a lesser time period). The number of visits is roughly equivalent to the number of different people that visit a site. This term is ambiguous unless the user defines it, since it could mean a user session or it could mean a unique visitor that day.

SEARCH ENGINE MARKETING

Description tag: An HTML tag used by Web page authors to provide a description for search engine listings.

Doorway domain: A domain used specifically to rank well in search engines for particular keywords, serving as an entry point through which visitors pass to the main domain.

Doorway page: A page made specifically to rank well in search engines for particular keywords, serving as an entry point through which visitors pass to the main content.

Invisible Web: The portion of the Web not accessible through Web search engines.

Keyword: A word used in a performing a search.

Keyword density: Keywords as a percentage of indexable text words.

Keyword research: The search for keywords related to your Web site, and the analysis of which ones yield the highest return on investment (ROI).

Keywords tag: META tag used to help define the primary keywords of a Web page.

Link popularity: A measure of the quantity and quality of sites that link to your site.

Link text: The text contained in (and sometimes near) a hyperlink.

Log file: File that records the activity on a Web server.

Manual submission: Adding a URL to the search engines individually by hand.

Meta tag generator: Tool that will output META tags based on input page information.

Meta tags: Tags to describe various aspects about a Web page.

Pay-per-click search engine: Search engine where results are ranked according to the bid amount, and advertisers are charged when a searcher clicks on the search listing.

Search engine optimization: The process of choosing targeted keyword phrases related to a site, and ensuring that the site places well when those keyword phrases are part of a Web search.

Search engine submission: The act of supplying a URL to a search engine in an attempt to make a search engine aware of a site or page.

Search spy: A perpetually refreshing page that provides a real-time view of actual Web searches.

Title tag: HTML tag used to define the text in the top line of a Web browser, also used by many search engines as the title of search listings.

Top 10: The top ten search engine results for a particular search term.

URL: Location of a resource on the Internet.

Volunteer directory: A Web directory staffed primarily by unpaid volunteer editors.

SEARCH ENGINES AND WEB DIRECTORIES

Search engine: A program that indexes documents, then attempts to match documents relevant to the users' search requests.

Metasearch engine: A search engine that displays results from multiple search engines.

Portal: A site featuring a suite of commonly used services, serving as a starting point and frequent gateway to the Web (Web portal) or a niche topic (vertical portal).

Web directory: Organized, categorized listings of Web sites.

AltaVista: Search engine located at **www.altavista.com**.

Ask Jeeves: Metasearch engine located at **www.askjeeves.com**.

DogPile: Metasearch engine located at **www.dogpile.com**.

Excite: Portal located at **www.excite.com**.

Fast Search: Search syndication company located at **www.fastsearch .com** and **www.fast.no**—also powers the search engine located at **www.alltheweb.com**.

Go Network: Defunct portal located at **www.go.com**.

Google: Search engine located at **www.google.com**.

Goto: Pay-per-click search engine that changed names and is now located at **www.overture.com**.

Inktomi: Search syndication company located at **www.inktomi.com**.

Ixquick: Metasearch engine located at **www.ixquick.com**.

Looksmart: Web directory located at **www.looksmart.com**.

Mamma: metasearch engine located at **www.mamma.com**.

MSN Search: Search destination at **search.msn.com**.

Northern Light Search: Search engine located at **www.northernlight.com**.

Raging Search: Search engine located at **www.raging.com**.

Yahoo!: Portal located at **www.yahoo.com**.

Zworks: Metasearch engine located at **www.zworks.com**.

WEB DESIGN AND MARKETING

Ad space: The space on a Web page available for advertisements.

ALT text: HTML attribute that provides alternative text when non-textual elements, typically images, cannot be displayed.

Animated GIF: A graphic in the GIF89a file format that creates the effect of animation by rotating through a series of static images.

Bookmark: A link stored in a Web browser for future reference.

Cascading style sheets (CSS): A data format used to separate style from structure on Web pages.

Favico: A small icon that is used by some browsers to identify a bookmarked Web site.

Flash: multimedia technology developed by Macromedia to allow much interactivity to fit in a relatively small file size.

Frames: A structure that allows for the dividing of a Web page into two or more independent parts.

Home page: The main page of a Web site.

JavaScript: A scripting language developed by Netscape and used to create interactive Web sites.

Linkrot: When Web pages previously accessible at a particular URL are no longer reachable at that URL due to movement or deletion of the pages.

Navigation: That which facilitates movement from one Web page to another Web page.

Shopping cart: Software used to make a site's product catalogue available for online ordering, whereby visitors may select, view, add, delete, and purchase merchandise.

Site search: Search functionality specific to one site.

Splash page: A branding page before the home page of a Web site.

Web browser: A software application that allows for the browsing of the World Wide Web.

Web design: The selection and coordination of available components to create the layout and structure of a Web page.

Web site usability: The ease with which visitors are able to use a Web site.

INDEX

112, 115, 119, 122, 132, 140, 147, 149, 151, 152, 153, 156, 169, 170, 177, 183, 184, 185, 201-203, 208, 210-213, 216-218, 220, 221, 231, 232, 234, 237, 241, 250, 253-257

C

Campaign 15, 18-20, 33, 40, 41, 47, 53, 57, 58, 61, 63, 68, 69, 72, 73, 76,-78, 80, 85, 87, 89-94, 96-99, 101-108, 110-112, 115, 116, 118-120, 123, 126, 130, 140, 142, 146, 148, 151, 153, 155, 174, 184, 187, 202, 208- 215, 218-227, 229, 236-243, 246, 248, 250, 251, 254, 256, 257

Cascading style sheets CSS 181

Click through 29, 65, 75, 84, 89, 96, 99, 101, 103, 129, 221

Client 24, 208, 219, 220, 224, 246, 250

Comment 176

Competition 36-38, 40, 101, 112, 113, 147, 208, 210, 216, 217, 226

Computer 61, 96, 161, 186, 223, 240

Consumer 41, 73, 198

Content 17, 19, 28-32, 51, 54, 57, 59- 61, 66, 72-74, 77, 83, 85, 87, 90, 94, 97, 107, 119, 122, 123, 126, 128, 133-135, 139, 147, 155-157, 159-162, 167-170, 172-182, 185, 191, 214, 218, 228, 229, 234, 236, 238, 243, 249, 250

Copyright 57, 173, 180

Crawler 155, 156, 159, 160, 170, 174, 186

Customer 19, 21, 25-27, 40, 41, 49, 50, 52, 56, 60, 62, 65, 68, 84, 101, 104, 105, 112, 115, 119, 137, 183, 206, 209, 215, 224, 247, 257

D

Description 86, 100, 101, 135, 156, 171-174, 176, 177, 198, 214, 229, 231

Design 15, 18, 19, 21, 23, 28, 41, 52, 63, 65, 149, 169, 171, 176, 177, 179, 181, 184, 186, 190, 201-203, 205, 207, 217, 220, 244, 254

Domain 59, 85, 113, 116, 232

E

Environment 36, 39

142, 143, 146, 149, 150,
153, 194, 202, 205, 206,
208, 209-215, 218, 220,
224, 225, 227, 230, 239,
240, 256, 257

Search engine 15, 17, 19-24, 30,
32, 39, 42, 45, 49, 52, 54,
55, 59, 60, 62-68, 71, 81,
85, 86, 101, 104, 105, 106,
112, 115, 117, 118, 135,
141, 142, 144, 147, 150,
152, 155, 156, 157, 159,
160, 161, 163, 168, 169,
170, 172, 175, 178-189,
193, 198, 201-203, 209-211,
213, 215, 217-220, 224,
227-230, 233, 252, 256, 257

Search engine optimization 19,
21, 30, 32, 39, 42, 45, 52,
54, 60, 68, 85, 86, 105, 112,
115, 168, 169, 170, 182,
183, 184, 185, 201, 224,
228

Service 25, 26, 36, 37, 40, 50, 52,
53, 54, 56, 66, 71, 113, 120,
123, 129, 147, 150, 151,
169, 171, 175, 179, 185,
188, 195, 198, 210, 211,
213, 215, 232, 236, 240,
241, 244, 247, 248, 252

Shockwave 28

Sites 15, 16, 21, 23-25, 29-31, 45,

48, 51, 54, 55, 58, 59, 64,
68, 72-74, 76, 80, 82, 90,
97, 106, 107, 112-114, 116,
123, 129, 135, 136, 140,
143, 146, 158-160, 166,
168, 170, 179, 181, 182,
186, 187, 190, 192, 199,
210-213, 215-217, 219, 224,
227-229, 231-235, 237, 242,
243, 247, 249

Software 24, 66, 68, 144, 151,
152, 157, 187, 190, 209,
212, 224, 233, 244, 245,
246, 247

Spam 39, 47, 257

Spider 155, 156, 159, 172, 173,
187

Strategy 15, 21, 41, 46, 47, 52,
142, 144, 146, 148, 150,
203, 206, 207, 208, 216,
219, 220, 224, 225, 226,
240, 251

T

Tactic 56

Technique 15, 90, 147, 161, 180,
224, 255

Text 23, 31, 55, 74, 82, 83, 92,
97, 106, 121, 122, 123, 126,
127, 128, 157, 158, 159,
162, 172, 173, 174, 175,
176, 177, 178, 180, 184,

DID YOU BORROW THIS COPY?

Have you been borrowing a copy of *The Complete Guide to Google Advertising — Including Tips, Tricks, & Strategies to Create a Winning Advertising Plan* from a friend, colleague, or library? Wouldn't you like your own copy for quick and easy reference? To order, photocopy the form below and send to:

Atlantic Publishing Company
1405 SW 6th Ave • Ocala, FL 34471-0640

YES!

Send me____copy(ies) of *The Complete Guide to Google Advertising — Including Tips, Tricks, & Strategies to Create a Winning Advertising Plan* (ISBN: 978-1-60138-045-6) for $24.95 plus $7.00 for shipping and handling.

Please Print

_____
Name

_____
Organization Name

_____
Address

_____
City, State, Zip

❏ My check or money order is enclosed. *Please make checks payable to Atlantic Publishing Company.*

❏ My purchase order is attached. *PO #* _____

www.atlantic-pub.com • e-mail: sales@atlantic-pub.com

Order toll-free 800-814-1132

FAX 352-622-1875

Atlantic Publishing Company
1405 SW 6th Ave • Ocala, FL 34471-0640

Add $7.00 for USPS shipping and handling. For Florida residents PLEASE add the appropriate sales tax for your county.